The Winter Garden

Rita Buchanan

Plants that offer color and beauty
in every season of the year

For information about permission to reproduce selections from this book,
write to Permissions, Houghton Mifflin Company, 215 Park Avenue South,
New York, New York 10003.

For information about this and other Houghton Mifflin trade
and reference books and multimedia products, visit The Bookstore at
Houghton Mifflin on the World Wide Web at http://www.hmco.com/trade/.

Taylor's Guide is a registered trademark of Houghton Mifflin Company.

Library of Congress Cataloging-in-Publication Data

Buchanan, Rita.
The winter garden / Rita Buchanan.
        p. cm. — (Taylor's weekend gardening guides)
    Includes bibliographical references (p.   ) and index.
    ISBN 0-395-82750-7
    1. Winter garden plants — United States. 2. Winter gardening — United States.
    I. Title. II. Series.
SB439.5.B83 1997
635.9′5 — dc21   97-10466

Printed in the United States of America

WCT 10 9 8 7 6 5 4 3 2 1

Book design by Deborah Fillion
Cover photograph © by David Cavagnaro

Frances Tenenbaum, Series Editor

HOUGHTON MIFFLIN COMPANY
Boston • New York 1997

Contents

This is a book for gardeners in northern and mountainous regions of the United States, where winter is the longest season. Throughout those areas, deciduous trees and shrubs are leafless for six to eight months. Many gardeners welcome the rest that winter allows. Since there aren't many chores to do outdoors, you have time to sit back, daydream, read books and catalogs, and simply stare out the window. What, though, do you see when you look at your garden in winter? Is it beautiful or boring?

A garden doesn't have to look barren just because it's winter. Winter is a dramatic season,

The simple geometry of this formal garden, with its boxwood hedges and latticework, makes a lovely sight in winter.

and a winter garden can be an engaging sight, rich with color, texture, and detail. There are plenty of hardy plants, large and small, that stand up to cold and snow and offer something special to enjoy during the winter months — evergreen foliage, distinctive bark or twigs, bright berries, or precocious flowers. This book features over 150 species and hundreds of cultivars of trees, shrubs, vines, grasses, perennials, and bulbs that could add beauty to your garden between November and April. All are hardy enough to survive sub-zero temperatures (many endure cold as extreme as twenty, thirty, or even forty degrees below zero) and come back year after year. Most of the plants are readily available at good local garden centers or nurseries, and the newer and rarer kinds can be purchased from major mail-order nurseries.

PLANNING FOR WINTER

If you were starting from scratch, you could reverse the usual priorities and design a garden with winter in mind. There are advantages to thinking this way. First, it reminds you to start with the basics and design a garden with clear lines, simple shapes, and balanced proportions. Winter reveals the basic design or "bones" of your garden — the layout of the paths and walkways; the contours and areas of the lawns and beds; the size and placement of the trees, shrubs, and hedges; use of structures such as fences, walls, raised beds, trellises, or arbors; and features such as benches, birdbaths, sculptures, or planters. In winter, you tend to step back from your garden and view it from indoors or from your car as you come and go. Looking from a distance helps you see the big picture, not just the details. If the "bones" of a garden are satisfying in winter, they'll make a good framework for the billowing foliage and flowers of summer.

Another important point is that choosing plants that look good in winter is likely to provide year-round interest, because most of the plants that look good in winter also have lovely flowers in spring or summer, colorful fall foliage, or other features. Even if they're simply a block of greenery, like a yew or arborvitae hedge, at least they are there to look at. By contrast, plants that are chosen for a brief floral display in summer may be nondescript or even absent the rest of the year. Perennial borders or annual flowerbeds look like bare ground for over half the year.

Designing an entire landscape from scratch is an uncommon opportunity. More often than not, you have to work around existing plants and features. You can always remodel an existing landscape, however, by pruning, thinning, or moving the best specimen trees and shrubs; dividing and rejuvenating the perennials and groundcovers; adding some fresh new plants; and repairing or replacing worn pavement or structures. Winter is a good time to plan this work, and you can remodel with winter in mind, considering changes and additions that will make your property more interesting throughout the whole year.

For example, instead of filling a whole bed with annual flowers every summer, you could plant an evergreen shrub and a few clumps of ornamental grasses in the center of the bed, leaving room for annuals around the edge. You might replace an overgrown maple or ash tree with a neat little Chinese dogwood that wouldn't cast so much shade on your garden and would have eye-catching bark in winter plus beautiful white flowers in summer and colorful fruit and foliage in fall. Around the base of the dogwood you could use some evergreen perennials such as hellebores, bergenias, or Christmas ferns as a groundcover. You could dig out a straggly privet or buckthorn hedge and plant a row of cheerful red-twig dogwoods, sparkling winterberry hollies, or early-blooming rhododendrons. On a south-facing bank where the soil dries out in summer so the grass turns brown (and is hard to mow anyway), plant drought-tolerant, low-growing evergreen junipers, bearberry, or sedums for a groundcover that looks good all year. Interplant with snowdrops, crocuses, and other spring bulbs; warmed by the sun, they bloom earlier than usual on a south-facing slope. Once you start looking, you'll spot many opportunities for improving your garden with plants that are beautiful in winter.

DEALING WITH WINTER'S WOES

As you know, winter isn't always as pretty as a calendar scene. It can be maddening to a gardener, because cold and snow are hard on plants. It's heartbreaking to watch an ice storm or blizzard snap or crush your prized trees and shrubs, or to wake up to a late spring frost that has turned your long-awaited magnolia and cherry blossoms into brown mush. There isn't much you can do to mitigate these calamities, but you can take steps to deal with normal winter conditions.

Cold-Hardiness. Over the last several decades, horticulturists have studied the winter survival of thousands of kinds of plants grown in gardens around the United States and Canada. They have also studied climate and weather records and devised a map that divides the region into eleven zones, based primarily on the average winter low temperatures. Most garden books, magazines, and nursery catalogs refer to the most recent edition of this map, which was published by the U.S. Department of Agriculture in 1990. For example, USDA Zone 5, where winter lows typically range from $-20°$ to $-10°F$, includes parts of the Rockies, and extends from eastern Colorado across the Midwest, along the south edge of the Great Lakes, and east into New England. Plants are rated according to the coldest zone in which they normally survive. Almost all of the plants in this book are hardy at least to USDA Zone 5. A few are hardy only to Zone 6 (winter lows of $-10°$ to $0°F$). Several are hardy to Zone 4 (lows of $-30°$ to $-20°F$), Zone 3 ($-40°$ to $-30°F$), or even Zone 2 ($-50°$ to $-40°F$). It's customary to list just one zone number for a plant to save space, but if a plant is rated Zone 4, for example, that doesn't mean it's recommended only for Zone 4. It means the plant should survive in Zone 4 and also in Zones 5, 6, 7, and so on.

Refer to the map on p. 113 or ask experienced gardeners in your neighborhood to find out what hardiness zone you live in and choose plants accordingly. Hardiness zone ratings are based on the average of many observations, and in general the system works well. Record-breaking cold spells or sudden and extreme temperature changes can kill otherwise hardy plants, but such severe weather happens only every once in a while. When it does, try again, since the plants deserve a second chance.

Plants that are normally hardy may die even in normal winters if they were previously stressed by drought, disease, or insect damage; if they were planted too late in the fall and didn't have time to get established; if the soil is too dry or stays frozen and the plant gets dehydrated; if the soil is waterlogged and the roots drown; or if there's not enough soil or mulch to cover the roots, so they freeze. If you lose a plant for one of these reasons, try to figure out what went wrong, then replace it with another of the same kind or try something else.

Don't be afraid to take a chance with a marginally hardy plant if it's something you really want to grow. Plants can survive one or two zones north of their regular zone if planted in a sheltered site surrounded by buildings that block the

A coating of fresh snow highlights the quiet beauty of a winter garden.

If you want to try growing a marginally hardy plant, choose a site protected by nearby trees, where snow blankets the ground from fall to spring.

wind and retain heat, underneath large evergreen trees that reduce radiative heat loss on cold nights, on a hillside where cold air flows down and away, or near a large body of water. When in doubt, pamper a cherished but perhaps tender plant by wrapping it with burlap, building a shelter around it, mounding soil around it, or mulching its roots with conifer boughs. Extra protection is especially helpful for the first few winters; once it's gotten established in your garden, a plant can tolerate more cold.

Plan Ahead. Anticipate the coming of winter and do what you can to maximize plant survival and minimize avoidable damage. Here are simple steps to take.

- Avoid planting valuable or brittle shrubs under the eaves of a house where snow and ice slide off the roof, or close to a road, driveway, or sidewalk where snow piles up from plowing and shoveling. For those locations, choose shrubs that can or should be pruned severely every spring, such as red-twig dogwood, shrub willows, spiraea, or potentilla; low-growing or prostrate groundcovers; or perennials and grasses that die down every winter and grow back quickly in spring.

- Don't fertilize or prune perennials or shrubs after midsummer, to avoid promoting a late spurt of tender new growth, which is liable to freeze. These plants are more likely to survive the winter if they slow down, stop growing, and "harden off" before hard frosts in fall.

- Plants that need well-drained soil are particularly sensitive to wetness during winter, when they are dormant. If your garden is soggy after a rain or when the snow melts in spring, you'll have to make raised beds for plants that require well-drained soil.

- When the soil freezes and thaws repeatedly, it tends to heave plants — especially shallow-rooted or recently planted perennials — out of the ground, making the plant much more liable to freeze or dry out. Prevent heaving by spreading a coarse-textured mulch such as conifer boughs, perennial stalks, pine needles, oak leaves, or loose hay or straw over the bed as soon as the ground has frozen. The purpose of this kind of mulch is not to prevent the soil from freezing, but to keep it frozen continually throughout the winter. Leave the mulch in place until the forsythias bloom in spring; don't remove it too soon.

- Bring terra cotta and glazed ceramic pots and planters into a basement or garage where they will be protected from frost, which is liable to crack them. Fiberglass, concrete, plastic, and wooden planters are usually weatherproof. Follow the manufacturer's advice for storing garden furniture, sculptures, and ornaments; some of these are frostproof, but others are likely to crack, fade, or mildew if left outdoors.

CHAPTER 1:

EVERGREENS

Gardeners take green for granted in the summer, but in the winter green foliage is a welcome sight. Evergreens add color to the dull gray, tan, and white winter landscape, and remind us of the growth that will resume in spring. In warm climates, many plants are evergreen. In Zones 6 and colder, your choices are limited to hardy conifers, a handful of broadleaf evergreen shrubs, and a few dozen kinds of evergreen perennials and groundcovers. Still, these are enough to provide a fascinating variety of foliage colors and textures, on plants of different sizes and shapes. Using evergreens alone, you can "paint" a garden scene that you'll enjoy looking at all year, especially in winter.

"Evergreens" come in all shades of green and in other colors, too. Conifers — trees and shrubs with needlelike or scalelike leaves — can be bright or dark green, blue-green, blue-gray, purplish, greenish yellow, gold, copper, bronze, or brown. Some are variegated, with splashes of white or gold on a green background. Many conifers change color in winter, then change back again in spring. Most conifers are fine-textured; they have lots of thin or small leaves, arranged close together.

Large and small conifers and sheared evergreen shrubs add year-round structure to this Japanese-style garden.

Broadleaf evergreens typically have thick, leathery leaves, but these can be tiny or large, dull or glossy, flat or curved, with smooth or toothed edges. Most broadleaf evergreens are medium or dark green in summer and fall, but some have variegated leaves marked with gold or white, and many kinds (plain or variegated) turn shades of red, purple, or bronze in cold weather. Evergreen perennials and groundcovers typically form low rosettes or mats of large or small leaves in all shades of green, gray, blue-green, red-purple, and gold.

Consider how much and what kind of snow you get when choosing which evergreens to plant. Dwarf shrubs and evergreen groundcovers are wonderful where snow is light or infrequent, but you'll lose sight of them for months where snow cover is continuous. If you regularly get lots of snow, grow some shrubs or trees that are large enough to not get buried. As you know from shoveling it, snow can be light or heavy. Dry, fluffy snow doesn't weigh down evergreens, but wet, heavy snow or a mixture of snow and freezing rain can cause major breakage. Some evergreens spring back up or sprout out again in spring if their limbs have been bent down or broken off, but others are permanently maimed. A good local nursery can tell you which evergreens are more or less resistant to snow damage in your climate.

CONIFERS

As well as having distinctive shapes and attractive needles, conifers provide shelter and seeds for songbirds. Individual conifer trees make distinguished lawn specimens. Planting a conifer windbreak or hedge will screen part or all of your property from cold winter winds. Slow-growing or dwarf conifers combine well with shrubs, grasses, and perennials in mixed beds and borders or foundation plantings.

In nature, most conifers mature into tall trees or large shrubs that would overwhelm many home landscapes. When choosing a conifer for your property, especially for planting near the house or other structures, measure the space that's available and choose a cultivar that won't outgrow it or one that grows slowly enough so that you can enjoy it for many years before it gets too large. The most common problem with conifers is that gardeners often don't allow enough space for them to develop naturally and achieve their full potential beauty.

Not all evergreens are green. This grouping of blue spruce, golden arborvitae, and spreading juniper provides a colorful winter display.

■ *Abies* spp. / Firs

DESCRIPTION: Firs are tall, slender, conical trees with short stiff needles and woody cones. Native to cool, moist northern or mountain climates, they grow well in similar settings but suffer through hot, dry summers. One of the most adaptable firs is *Abies concolor,* white fir, which has 2-inch, blue-green needles that can be almost as "blue" as those of the Colorado blue spruce. It tolerates summer heat and dry soil better than other firs and eventually grows quite large, to 50 feet or taller. For smaller gardens, consider the dwarf balsam fir, *A. balsamea* 'Nana' (flat, dark green needles; grows 2 to 4 feet tall and wide), or the prostrate form of Korean fir, *A. koreana* 'Prostrate Beauty' (curved green-and-silver needles; slowly spreads to 2 feet tall, 6 feet wide or wider). All are hardy to Zone 4.

CULTURE: Full or part sun. Well-drained soil with a layer of mulch and regular watering during dry spells. Pruning is not required.

■ *Chamaecyparis* spp. / False cypresses

DESCRIPTION: In the wild these are big trees, but there are scores of dwarf cultivars just right for small gardens. The hardiest (Zone 5, sometimes Zone 4) and most widely adapted cultivars are selections of *Chamaecyparis obtusa,* Hinoki cypress; *C. pisifera,* Sawara cypress; and *C. thyoides,* Atlantic white cedar. These can be upright and conical or low and rounded, with bright or dark green, blue-green, blue-gray, gold, or variegated foliage in a wide range of textures — scaly, stringy, furry, prickly, or mossy. Growth rate and mature size vary. Most dwarfs grow only a few inches a year. Upright forms eventually reach 10 to 15 feet tall; mounded types stay 1 to 3 feet tall.

CULTURE: Part sun in summer, shade in winter. Moist, fertile, well-drained soil with a layer of mulch and regular watering during dry spells. Can be sheared or pruned if you choose.

■ *Juniperus* spp. / Junipers

DESCRIPTION: Junipers are popular because they are so varied and easy to grow. They can be upright trees with distinct trunks and slender crowns, broad bushy shrubs, or low groundcovers. In any form, they have prickly or scaly foliage in various shades of green, blue-green, or blue-gray. Female plants bear little blue fruits. The following cultivars are some of the most attractive and popular.

Hinoki cypress 'Crippsii' (Chamaecyparis obtusa) *has curly sprays of bright golden foliage. It grows slowly; this plant is many decades old.*

First, some upright forms. *Juniperus scopulorum* 'Pathfinder' and 'Wichita Blue' both form broad cones, up to 15 feet tall, with silvery blue foliage. Zone 4. *J. chinensis* 'Robusta Green' and 'Torulosa' both are upright, to 10 feet or taller, with dense, irregular, twisted growth and bright green foliage. Zone 5.

Among the best mid-size junipers are *J. chinensis* 'Sea Green', 30 inches tall, with feathery green foliage on arching shoots, and the compact, gold, and blue forms of Pfitzer juniper, *J. chinensis* 'Pfitzerana', which all grow 2 to 3 feet tall and 4 to 6 feet wide. Zone 4.

For groundcovers, consider 'Bar Harbor', 'Blue Chip', 'Wiltonii', or 'Blue Rug', all cultivars of *J. horizontalis,* with colorful blue-gray or blue-silver foliage that turns purplish in winter, or 'Mother Lode', with needles that are bright yellow in summer, golden orange in fall, purplish in winter. All have creeping stems that hug the ground and spread 4 to 6 feet or wider. Zone 3. *J. procumbens* 'Nana' has creeping stems that spread to 6 feet or wider, with mossy-looking but prickly textured, pale green foliage. Zone 5. *J. sabina* 'Arcadia' and 'Broadmoor' form mounds or patches, 1 to 2 feet tall and 4 to 6 feet wide, of short arching stems with feathery, bright green foliage. Zone 3. *J. squamata* 'Blue Carpet' and 'Blue Star' form irregular mounds or mats, 1 to 2 feet tall and 3 feet wide or wider, with sparkling silver-blue needles. Zone 4.

CULTURE: All junipers do best with full sun. They need well-drained soil and cannot tolerate wet soil or excess humidity. Under suitable conditions they are trouble-free. Cultivars that are the right size and shape for their site rarely need pruning, but if it is needed, junipers can be pruned annually in early summer.

■ *Microbiota decussata* / **Siberian cypress**

DESCRIPTION: An unusual conifer that tolerates shade and spreads to form a groundcover. It's a short, broad plant, under 1 foot tall and 4 to 6 feet wide, with limbs that spread horizontally and soft feathery foliage that is bright green in summer, bronze or brown in winter. Zone 3.

CULTURE: Sun or shade. Moist, well-drained soil. Care-free.

■ *Picea* spp. / **Spruces**

DESCRIPTION: Spruces have a perfect Christmas-tree shape and are adaptable and easy to grow. Eventually they grow too large for most lots and dominate the

'Sea Green' juniper (Juniperus chinensis) *is a spreading shrub about 30 inches tall that keeps its bright green foliage color all winter.*

'Bar Harbor' juniper (Juniperus horizontalis) *is an excellent groundcover for sunny slopes. During the coldest months, the foliage changes from this blue color to a purplish hue.*

house, but you can enjoy a regular spruce for many years before it overwhelms the garden, or you could choose a dwarf cultivar and admire it for decades. Spruces have stiff, prickly needles and oblong woody cones with seeds that attract birds. Norway spruce, *Picea abies,* with dark green needles and drooping branchlets, and Colorado blue spruce, *P. pungens,* with blue or blue-green needles, are the most popular spruces, available in many dwarf or prostrate cultivars as well as the standard full-size (50 feet or taller) forms. The dwarf Alberta spruce, *P. glauca* 'Conica', has an upright conical shape but grows slowly, rarely exceeding 8 to 10 feet tall, so it's a good long-term garden investment. It has very dense, fine-textured, prickly, pale green foliage. Less common but equally adaptable and even more beautiful are the Serbian spruce, *P. omorika,* and Oriental spruce,

The Colorado blue spruce (Picea pungens) *grows fast, has a perfect Christmas-tree shape, and provides shelter and seeds for many songbirds.*

P. orientalis, which grow as tall but not as wide as blue or Norway spruces, and have dense, dark green foliage. All of these spruces are hardy to Zone 4.

CULTURE: Full sun. Moist, well-drained soil. Subject to insect attacks in some regions but generally trouble-free. No pruning required.

■ *Pinus* spp. / Pines

DESCRIPTION: Like most conifers, young pine trees have a Christmas-tree shape, but as they mature pines typically develop an open crown that can be very picturesque. Unlike other conifers, pines look distinguished, not silly, with their lower limbs removed so that you can garden or simply walk underneath, and many pines have attractive bark. Pines have short or long, soft or stiff needles in

Most pines grow into large trees, but the mugo pine (Pinus mugo) *is a small, bushy plant.*

various shades of green (occasionally blue-green or yellow-green) and big woody cones with seeds that attract chickadees and other songbirds.

Native pines such as eastern white pine, *Pinus strobus;* red pine (often called Norway pine, although it's native to the northern Great Lakes region), *P. resinosa;* and ponderosa or western yellow pine, *P. ponderosa,* are justly popular where they grow wild and often can be grown successfully outside those regions. All mature into large trees, 60 feet or taller.

Dwarf, shrub-sized pines make fine specimens for smaller gardens or in foundation plantings. There are many excellent dwarf cultivars of the eastern white pine and also of the Scots pine, *P. sylvestris.* The popular mugo or Swiss mountain pine, *P. mugo,* grows naturally into a low, mounded shape, and its dwarf forms are especially compact. In choosing any pine, full-size or dwarf, ask a local nursery for advice about how fast it will grow, how big it will get, and whether it's susceptible to any local disease or insect problems. All of the pines named here are hardy to Zone 4.

CULTURE: All pines grow best in full sun and well-drained soil. In general, established pines require no care, but you can prune them if you want to by cutting back the new shoots in early summer, after they have elongated but before the wood hardens.

■ *Pseudotsuga menziesii* / **Douglas fir**

DESCRIPTION: This native of the western mountains grows like spruces do but has less rigid branches and softer needles. Like spruces, Douglas fir seedlings generally grow fast and eventually get too large for most gardens. However, selected cultivars with blue foliage or weeping limbs are slower growing, smaller, and very attractive. Zone 4.

CULTURE: Full or part sun. Well-drained garden soil. Prone to certain insects and diseases but generally trouble-free.

■ *Taxus* spp. / **Yews**

DESCRIPTION: Most yews are slow-growing small trees that can reach 25 feet tall and wide or larger, with short flat dark green needles. Female plants bear fleshy red fruits that are showy for many weeks in late fall and winter. Although yews respond particularly well to pruning, it's much more convenient to main-

Conifers such as these Austrian pines (Pinus nigra) *bend under the weight of a heavy snow load, but they'll spring back up when the snow melts.*

'Nana' yew (Taxus cuspidata) *forms a compact, rounded shrub that needs little if any pruning.*

tain a cultivar that develops naturally to the size and shape you want. Consider also winter foliage color (some yews turn a dirty tan or brown in winter) and hardiness when choosing a yew. The following cultivars are widely grown, retain their green color in winter, and are hardy to Zone 4. *Taxus cuspidata* 'Greenwave' forms a low mound with arching branches. *T. cuspidata* 'Nana' has very dense, low growth and spreads to about twice as wide as it is tall. *T. × media* 'Hatfieldii' forms a broad upright pyramid, grows slowly to about 10 feet tall, and makes a large specimen tree or wide hedge. *T. × media* 'Hicksii' is narrow and columnar, grows quickly to about 10 feet tall, and makes a good narrow hedge. There are many other fine yews, especially for gardens in Zones 5 and 6.

CULTURE: Yews tolerate shade better than most conifers and grow well on the north side of a building. They also thrive in full sun. Well-drained soil is the most important consideration, as yews cannot tolerate waterlogged conditions. Appropriately chosen cultivars are care-free. If you need to control overly vigorous plants or want to shape formal specimens or hedges, shear back the new growth in early summer, before it has hardened.

- *Thuja* spp. / Arborvitae

DESCRIPTION: Cultivars of American arborvitae, *Thuja occidentalis,* make excellent specimens, hedges, and foundation plantings. They grow upright, with conical or rounded profiles, and typically have flat sprays of fragrant, glossy foliage and small woody cones. 'Emerald' and 'Wintergreen' are thin, almost columnar when young; 'Nigra' and 'Techny' are broader. All grow much taller than their width and have bright or dark green foliage that retains its color in winter. 'Woodwardii' or globe arborvitae has a rounded shape, up to 8 feet tall and wide, and is green in summer but turns bronze in winter. 'Hetz Midget' looks like a green ball and takes years to grow 3 feet tall and wide. 'Aurea' and 'Rhein-

'Aurea' arborvitae (Thuja occidentalis) *is an upright shrub 3 to 5 feet tall with fragrant foliage that is bright gold in summer and golden bronze in winter.*

TIPS FOR SUCCESS

Deer are strongly attracted to some evergreens, especially in snowy winters when other food is limited. Fencing your garden, leaving a dog outside day and night, putting bird net over individual plants, and spraying plants with a repellent offer some protection, but if the deer population is high in your area, it's a good idea to choose plants accordingly.

Deer eagerly strip the foliage from yews *(Taxus)*, arborvitae *(Thuja)*, winter creeper *(Euonymus fortunei cvs.)*, and rhododendrons and azaleas *(Rhododendron)*. Depending on how hungry they are, they also nibble on false cypresses *(Chamaecyparis)*, junipers *(Juniperus)*, hemlocks *(Tsuga)*, and mountain laurel *(Kalmia latifolia)*. Deer normally avoid firs *(Abies)*, spruces *(Picea)*, pines *(Pinus)*, boxwoods *(Buxus)*, hollies *(Ilex)*, Oregon grape and holly grape *(Mahonia)*, and andromedas *(Pieris)*.

gold' are rounded or conical, 3 to 5 feet tall, with foliage that is gold in summer, bronze in winter. All are hardy to Zone 4.

Western arborvitae, *T. plicata,* grows quickly into a very attractive conical tree, eventually reaching 50 feet or taller, with fernlike foliage that is green in summer, golden brown in winter. Zone 5. Cultivars of Oriental arborvitae, *T. orientalis,* do well across the southern United States but are not hardy north of Zone 6.

CULTURE: Full or part sun. Average soil with regular watering during dry spells. American and western arborvitaes adapt well to moist or heavy soils but not to dry or sandy sites. Arborvitaes can be pruned but don't require it. They usually need protection from winter storm damage. Ice storms or heavy wet snows can spread the leaders apart and bend them over. Prevent this by using wire or rot-resistant twine to tie the leaders together in several places. Don't tie too tightly, and replace the ties every few years so they don't girdle the growing stems.

■ *Tsuga* spp. / Hemlocks

DESCRIPTION: Canada hemlock, *Tsuga canadensis,* is one of the most graceful conifers. It normally grows into a large tree with relaxed, swaying branches and soft, fine-textured, dark green foliage, but it can be sheared for use as a large hedge. There are slow-growing, weeping cultivars that spread wider than tall; dwarf mounded or prostrate forms; and a few kinds with gold- or white-variegated foliage. All are hardy to Zone 4 but intolerant of hot, dry summers. The Carolina hemlock, *T. caroliniana,* looks similar to Canada hemlock but has stiffer limbs. It's more tolerant of exposed sites and warm summer weather. Hardy to Zone 5.

CULTURE: Part shade. Canada hemlock prefers a north or east exposure that provides some sun in summer and shade in winter. Hemlocks need cool, rich, moist, well-drained, acidic soil with a thick layer of organic mulch and regular watering during dry spells. They make beautiful specimens where the soil and climate are suitable but aren't recommended otherwise.

Canada hemlock is a graceful conifer with soft needles that stay bright green all winter.

Broadleaf Evergreen Shrubs

These versatile shrubs are indispensable for foundation plantings, hedges, mixed borders, and lawn specimens. Some are dwarf or slow-growing plants that never get more than a few feet tall or wide. Others reach 10 feet or taller and may become treelike. Almost all can be sheared or clipped into formal shapes if you choose. Left alone, their natural shapes may be rounded, conical, spreading, or angular and picturesque. Along with their colorful foliage and robust shapes, rhododendrons, mountain laurels, andromedas, and some other hardy evergreen shrubs also have beautiful flowers.

When choosing broadleaf evergreens, consider cold-hardiness first. If you plant one of these shrubs in a climate that's too severe, it may freeze to the ground and never recover. Next, evaluate the soil where you want to plant the shrub. Many of the shrubs listed here require well-drained, acid soil. They can't tolerate heavy clay, lime-bearing rocks, or lime leaching from a concrete house foundation, so you have to build raised beds and amend the soil with lots of peat moss and composted pine bark before planting if these are present. Flower color, ultimate size, rate of growth, and susceptibility to local pest and disease problems are other points to consider before buying a plant.

■ *Buxus* spp. / Boxwoods

DESCRIPTION: There are many fine cultivars of boxwood, with several traits in common: all have glossy rounded leaves, inconspicuous but fragrant flowers in spring, upright trunks, dense branches, and a plump profile. Cultivars differ, though, in ultimate size (3 to 20 feet tall and wide), rate of growth (from about 1 to 6 inches per year), hardiness (Zones 6, 5, or 4), and winter color (some stay rich green while others turn dull greenish purple, bright coppery gold, or dingy tan or brown). Ask about all these factors when choosing boxwood plants at a nursery. 'Green Velvet', 'Green Mound', 'Wintergreen', 'Winter Beauty', and most other cultivars with the words "green" or "winter" in their names are compact and hardy, and stay green all year.

CULTURE: Full or part sun. Well-drained soil. Boxwoods have shallow roots that need special attention. Apply mulch to keep them from heat, cold, and dryness, leaving an open space around the trunk to prevent stem rot. Be careful when

All kinds of boxwood (Buxus) *have dense, compact growth and fine-textured foliage.*

weeding, and never cultivate in the root zone. Boxwoods develop pleasant, rounded contours naturally; you can prune or shear them into formal shapes if you choose.

- *Cercocarpus ledifolius* / **Curl-leaf mountain mahogany**

  DESCRIPTION: A hardy shrub native to the western mountains, with picturesque angular branching growth; small, stiff, aromatic leaves, dark green above and silvery below; and silver-plumed seedheads in late summer and fall. Grows 10 to 20 feet tall and wide. Zone 5 or 4.

Euonymus 'Radicans' (Euonymus fortunei) *is a shrubby vine with glossy evergreen leaves and clusters of orange berries. It's a good vine to train up a tree trunk or grow against a wall.*

CULTURE: Full or part sun. Needs well-drained soil; tolerates gravelly or sandy sites. Makes a good windbreak or screen or can be clipped for a hedge or pruned into a specimen tree.

- *Euonymus fortunei* / **Euonymus, winter creeper**

DESCRIPTION: Dozens of cultivars have been selected from this versatile, adaptable evergreen. Some have fairly stiff stems and grow upright; others have drooping or trailing stems. The glossy, thick-textured leaves can be small or large, plain green or variegated. 'Sarcoxie' and var. *vegetus* are both upright forms, usu-

Euonymus 'Emerald 'n' Gold' (Euonymus fortunei) *is a low shrub with small leathery leaves that are dull gold in winter but turn a fresh bright yellow in early spring, as shown here.*

ally 4 to 6 feet tall, with thick, glossy, dark green leaves and clusters of small orange berries in fall and early winter. 'Green Lane' is also upright and shrubby but has larger, rounded, plain green leaves. 'Goldsplash' and 'Sunsplash' are small (2 to 4 feet tall and wide), rounded shrubs with stiff stems and green-and-yellow leaves. 'Emerald Gaiety' and 'Emerald 'n' Gold' are low, broad shrubs with supple stems and small green-and-white or green-and-yellow leaves. Specimens of any of these cultivars often become vinelike after growing in the same place for several years. If there is a tree or building nearby, they'll cling to it and grow 20 to 40 feet tall. Zone 5.

CULTURE: Sun or shade. Any well-drained soil. Euonymus is easy to grow and generally care-free, but it is susceptible to scale insects, and severe infestations can be fatal. Check often and spray with horticultural oil if needed. Prune anytime to control size and shape.

■ *Ilex* spp. / Hollies

DESCRIPTION: With their rich dark foliage and dense bushy habits, evergreen hollies are indispensable for the winter garden. In addition, female plants produce berries if there's a male nearby (see p. 84). Cultivars of *Ilex crenata,* Japanese holly, form mounds or cones 3 to 6 feet tall and wide. They have small dark green leaves with serrated edges and inconspicuous black berries. Zone 6 or 5. The native inkberry, *I. glabra,* has similar foliage and berries but grows upright, to 4 to 8 feet tall, and often gets leggy at the base. Zone 5 or 4.

'Blue Prince', 'Blue Princess', and other 'Blue' cultivars of *I.* × *meserveae* have spiny, dark blue-green leaves and purple stems. Most develop a leader and grow into upright pyramids. The related 'China Boy' and 'China Girl' have spiny, bright green foliage, yellow stems, and more rounded profiles. All can reach 8 to 15 feet tall. Female plants bear lots of bright red berries. Zone 5.

American holly, *I. opaca,* grows as an upright, open tree in the wild, with dull olive-green spiny foliage. Cultivars such as 'Greenleaf' and 'Jersey Princess' have bright green leaves and a dense conical growth habit, slowly reaching 20 feet or taller. Berries are red, or sometimes yellow. Zone 6 or 5.

Longstalk holly, *I. pedunculosa,* has spineless leaves that resemble mountain laurel, tiny red berries that dangle on stalks, and a graceful, bushy habit; it reaches about 20 feet tall. Zone 6 or 5.

American holly (Ilex opaca) *is a neat, slow-growing tree with spiny evergreen leaves and bright red berries. There are many fine cultivars.*

CULTURE: Part sun is best for most evergreen hollies, especially in winter, when full sun can scorch the leaves. Most prefer slightly acidic, well-drained, moist soil topped with a thick layer of composted leaves, bark chips, or other organic mulch. Prune anytime to control size and shape.

- *Kalmia latifolia* / **Mountain laurel**

DESCRIPTION: Mountain laurel grows wild throughout the Appalachians, forming vast thickets. Dozens of cultivars have been selected for garden use. Most grow upright, 6 to 10 feet tall. Some are compact and rounded, 3 to 6 feet tall. All have shiny, pointed leaves; color ranges from dark green to olive to yellowish green, depending on the cultivar and growing conditions. In bloom, mountain laurels are as showy as azaleas or rhododendrons. They have round clusters of red

or pink buds that open into cup-shaped red, pink, or white flowers. The display lasts for a few weeks in June. Zone 5.

CULTURE: Sun or shade. The more sun, the more flowers and the faster the plant grows. The more shade, the prettier the foliage but the slower it grows. Mountain laurel needs fertile, acid, moist, well-drained soil. Amend average garden soil with peat moss and mulch with pine needles or composted leaves. Snap off flowerheads immediately after the petals drop; if you let the seeds develop, the plant will bloom only in alternate years.

Mountain laurel (Kalmia latifolia) *is a versatile shrub that adapts to sunny or shady sites and bears showy clusters of white or pink flowers in early summer.*

■ *Leucothoe* spp. / Leucothoes

DESCRIPTION: These mounded shrubs have arching limbs lined with lovely foliage. The glossy pointed leaves are dark green in summer and usually turn burgundy in winter. Clusters of small white flowers open in late spring. *Leucothoe axillaris,* coast leucothoe, grows 2 to 4 feet tall, 3 to 5 feet wide. Zone 6. *L. fontanesiana,* drooping leucothoe, grows 3 to 6 feet tall and wide. Zone 5.

CULTURE: Part sun or shade. Fertile, acid, moist, well-drained soil. Amend average garden soil with peat moss and mulch with pine needles or composted

Winter Protection for Broadleaf Evergreens

Even though they may be hardy to cold temperatures, broadleaf evergreens can be stressed by dry winds and bright sun in winter. When the ground is frozen, roots can't replace water lost through the leaves. As a result, the leaves and even the twigs may die back, turning tan or brown as they do, and drop off in spring, leaving the plant bare for a while before new growth appears. This looks ugly and it weakens the plant, so take suitable steps to minimize winter stress.

■ Plant broadleaf evergreen shrubs on the north or east side of a building or structure. Avoid planting evergreens on the south or west side, where the temperature gets quite warm on sunny afternoons, then drops abruptly at sunset. Sudden temperature fluctuations harm plants.

■ Plant shrubs under deciduous trees, whose bare limbs cast enough shade to prevent winter sunburn.

■ Plant a windbreak or build a fence to protect your garden from prevailing winter winds.

■ Spray evergreen shrubs with an antitranspirant such as Wiltpruf, following the directions on the label.

■ Protect individual shrubs from sun and wind by building a cage of stakes and burlap around them. Leave the top open for air circulation.

■ If rainfall is insufficient, water enough to thoroughly soak the soil around each shrub before the ground freezes.

Japanese andromeda (Pieris japonica) *matures into a tall, broad shrub with shiny green foliage. Clusters of reddish flower buds form in fall. They are colorful all winter and open into white flowers in spring.*

leaves. Water during dry spells. Space plants far enough apart for good air circulation to reduce the risk of leaf-spot diseases. Prune after flowering, if desired.

■ *Mahonia* spp. / Oregon grape, holly grape

DESCRIPTION: Unrelated to grapes or hollies, these are distinctive, hardy, native shrubs. *Mahonia aquifolium,* Oregon grape, forms an erect clump 4 to 8 feet tall, with stiff, unbranched stems. Zone 5. *M. repens,* creeping holly grape, stays under 1 foot tall and spreads slowly to form a patch. Zone 4. Both have compound leaves with hollylike leaflets that are stiff-textured with spiny edges, dark green in summer and purple-bronze in winter. Clusters of fragrant, golden flowers last for a few weeks in spring; small, edible blue berries last for months in late summer and fall.

CULTURE: These plants do best on the north or east side of a building or screen, where there is part sun in summer but shelter from winter sun and wind. On exposed sites, the leaves turn brown and drop off, and the stems may freeze. Well-drained soil. Cut back old, tattered, or too-tall stems in early spring.

■ *Pieris* spp. / Andromedas

DESCRIPTION: Andromedas are bushy, upright shrubs with glossy, pointed leaves. Clusters of reddish buds are conspicuous all winter and open into tiny, bell-shaped flowers in early spring. There are dozens of cultivars of Japanese andromeda, *Pieris japonica;* most grow 6 to 12 feet tall. The flowers can be white, pink, or rosy. The leaves unfold in bright shades of gold, red, or bronze, then darken to a medium or dull green the rest of the year. Zone 6. Mountain andromeda, *P. floribunda,* and the hybrid 'Brouwer's Beauty' are less common at nurseries, but more compact (3 to 6 feet tall) and hardy to Zone 5. Both have olive or medium green leaves and white flowers.

CULTURE: Part sun. Need fertile, moist, well-drained, acid soil. Amend average garden soil with peat moss and mulch with pine needles or composted leaves. Water regularly during summer dry spells. Snap off the flowerheads as soon as the petals fade and do any desired pruning at the same time. Andromedas are susceptible to lacebugs, and severe infestations can be fatal. Check often and spray with horticultural oil if needed.

- *Rhododendron* spp. / Rhododendrons

DESCRIPTION: Beloved for their flowers, hardy rhododendrons are also important foliage plants, valuable for foundation plantings, hedges, screening, and specimens. The leaves can be large or small, glossy or dull, flat or curled. Generally, the small-leaved types are hardier and look better in severe weather; their leaves typically turn purple or bronze in winter. Large-leaved rhododendrons keep their dark green color in winter, but the leaves curl and droop in a pitiful way when air temperature drops much below freezing. Foliage quality and hardiness vary among cultivars, so consider these factors as well as the flowers when choosing which rhododendrons to plant. Many cultivars are hardy in Zone 5, some in Zone 4.

CULTURE: See p. 103.

- *Viburnum* spp. / Viburnums

DESCRIPTION: Several viburnums are evergreen in mild climates, but only a few kinds keep their leaves in cold winters. The following are semi-evergreen in Zone 5; they usually hold their leaves through December but rarely until spring. Their open habit offers a distinct contrast to the dense growth of most hardy evergreens. *Viburnum × pragense* has narrow, shiny, dark green leaves. *V. × rhytidophylloides* 'Allegheny' and 'Willowwood' both have large, rough-textured, gray-green leaves. All three of these viburnums are fairly fast-growing and can reach 10 feet tall and wide, with erect or arching stems, and bear rounded clusters of creamy white flowers in spring and dark red berries in fall. Zone 5.

One of the nicest viburnums is a new hybrid, 'Conoy'. Although it's not common at nurseries yet, it should be soon. It grows 4 to 5 feet tall and 5 to 8 feet wide, with small, oval, glossy leaves that are dark green in summer and purplish in winter. It has clusters of fragrant white flowers in late spring and red berries in fall. Hardy on sheltered sites in Zone 5.

CULTURE: Full or part sun. Fertile, moist, well-drained soil. Use mulch and water during dry spells to keep the roots moist. Prune young plants hard for the first few years to force them to branch out near the base. Prune older plants by removing weak or crowded stems at ground level. Heavy snows in early winter can break the limbs, and hard frosts in late spring can kill the tips of the shoots. In either case, if you remove the damaged parts the plant will soon recover.

A light spring snow dusts this mixed planting of evergreen rhododendrons and azaleas, highlighting their rounded shapes.

This variegated form of yucca or bear grass (Yucca filamentosa), *with green-and-gold striped leaves, makes a distinctive specimen in any season.*

■ *Yucca* spp. / Yucca, bear grass

DESCRIPTION: A unique evergreen that spreads slowly to form a wide patch with many rosettes of sword-shaped leaves, 2 feet long, with sharp tips and curly fibers along the edges. *Yucca filamentosa* and *Y. flaccida,* the most commonly cultivated species, usually have gray-green leaves. There are variegated cultivars whose leaves have creamy white or golden yellow stripes. All have tall branched stalks of large, waxy white flowers in June. Zone 5.

CULTURE: Full sun. Well-drained soil. Care-free; just remove old flower stalks and dead leaves from time to time.

Semi-evergreen Herbs

Although their fragrance and flavor are diminished in cold weather, several herbs hold their leaves at least partway into the winter. Parsley *(Petroselinum crispum)* stays green and good throughout the fall. Shrubby herbs such as wormwood and southernwood *(Artemisia* spp.), lavender *(Lavandula)*, garden sage *(Salvia officinalis)*, germander *(Teucrium)*, and thyme *(Thymus)* stand up through several hard frosts or early snows before they get frozen or flattened.

If you cut away the old stalks in fall, you usually find a tuft of new foliage at the base of yarrow *(Achillea)*, calamint *(Calamintha)*, horehound *(Marrubium)*, lemon balm *(Melissa)*, catmint *(Nepeta)*, and oregano *(Origanum)*. This basal foliage lasts all winter, ready to resume growth in early spring. Chives *(Allium schoenoprasum)* disappears in winter but is one of the first herbs you can pick in spring.

Many popular herbs such as English lavender (Lavandula angustifolia), *shown here in late November, hold their leaves at least partway through the winter.*

Low-Growing Evergreen Plants

The following small shrubs, perennials, and ferns all have evergreen or semi-evergreen foliage. Use them as groundcovers, along the edge of paths and walkways, in permanent outdoor planters, or as specimens in mixed beds and borders. Because they're short, these plants will sometimes be hidden by snow, but when you can see them, you'll enjoy them.

- *Ajuga reptans* / **Ajuga or bugle weed**

Semi-evergreen. A prostrate perennial with glossy leaves and very showy flower spikes 6 inches tall in late spring. There are many cultivars, differing in leaf color (green, bronze, purple, or variegated); leaf size (1 to 8 inches long); leaf texture (smooth, ruffled, or crinkled); habit (some kinds spread quickly by runners and make a big patch, others stay in compact clumps); and flower color (most forms have sky blue flowers, but some have pink or white). All prefer part shade and moist, well-drained soil. Zone 4.

The evergreen leaves of ajuga 'Bronze Beauty' (Ajuga reptans) *are etched with frost on a cold December morning.*

- *Andromeda polifolia* / **Bog rosemary**

Evergreen. A small shrub (1 foot tall, 2 to 3 feet wide) with slender leaves (like the herb rosemary) that are gray-green in summer, purple in winter, and clusters of small white or pale pink flowers in late spring. It needs cool, moist, acid soil amended with plenty of peat moss. Water weekly during dry spells. Zone 3. Cumberland rosemary, *Conradina verticillata,* is unrelated but is also a small native shrub with evergreen, rosemary-like foliage and pink flowers in spring. It needs a sunny site with sandy, well-drained soil and is hardy to Zone 5.

- *Arctostaphylos uva-ursi* / **Bearberry or kinnikinnick**

Evergreen. An excellent groundcover with woody stems and small, rounded, leathery leaves that are bright green in summer, turning maroon or bronze in winter. It has small pink flowers in spring and red berries in fall. 'Big Bear', 'Massachusetts', and 'Vancouver Jade' are especially attractive cultivars that grow just a few inches tall but spread several feet wide. Full or part sun. Soil must be well-drained; bearberry does well on slopes or in raised planters. Zone 4.

- *Asarum europaeum* / **European wild ginger**

An evergreen perennial with glossy heart-shaped leaves. Grows 4 to 6 inches tall and slowly spreads to form a mat 1 to 3 feet wide. Part or full shade. Rich, moist, well-drained soil. Zone 5.

- *Bergenia cordifolia* / **Heartleaf bergenia**

An evergreen perennial. Forms clumps of large, thick, cabbagelike leaves that turn from green to garnet red in cold weather. Clusters of pink or white flowers appear in early spring. Grows about 1 foot tall, spreads to 2 feet wide. Sun or part shade. Average or moist soil. Zone 3.

- *Calluna vulgaris* / **Heather**

Evergreen. A small shrub with wiry stems and tiny leaves. There are dozens of cultivars, varying in growth habit (most are 1 to 3 feet tall and 1 to 3 feet wide; they can be upright or spreading); foliage color (gray, light or dark green, or gold in summer; gray, green, gold, red, purplish, or bronze in winter); flower color (white, pink, lavender, or lilac); and flowering time (July to November). If you

can grow one, you can grow them all, and a collection of heathers makes a beautiful, low-maintenance, tapestry-like planting. All need full sun and well-drained acid soil. Heathers thrive in raised or mounded-up beds where the soil has been amended with plenty of peat moss and sand or gravel. Prune in early spring, cutting back the previous year's growth by about one-third. Zone 4.

See p. 97 for more information about heaths (*Erica* spp.), which combine well with heathers, blooming in late winter and early spring.

■ *Dianthus* / Pinks

Evergreen perennials with grassy-textured blue-green or blue-gray foliage. There are dozens of cultivars with single or double flowers in various shades of pink, rose, and white, typically with a spicy fragrance. Some kinds form a very compact mound of foliage, others make a loose mat. Foliage is usually 2 to 6 inches tall, flower stalks 4 to 12 inches tall. Full sun. Well-drained soil. Most pinks are hardy to Zone 4.

■ *Dryopteris marginalis* / Marginal shield fern or leatherwood fern

Evergreen. A native fern that forms loose clumps of fine-cut, medium green fronds about 2 feet tall. Part sun or shade. Moist, well-drained soil. Zone 3.

■ *Epimedium* / Bishop's hat

A semi-evergreen perennial with very attractive foliage. The stiff, papery, heart-shaped leaflets turn from dark green to purplish in cold weather. Small white, yellow, pink, or red flowers appear in spring. There are many cultivars; most grow 8 to 12 inches tall and spread slowly to form a dense patch. Part or full shade. Rich, moist, well-drained soil. Zone 5.

■ *Euonymus fortunei* / Winter creeper

Evergreen. The following cultivars are vining, not shrubby. They can climb a tree or wall but are usually used as groundcovers or in mixed plantings. *Euonymus fortunei* 'Coloratus' has leathery oblong leaves that are dark green in summer, purple-bronze in winter. Space plants 2 feet apart to make a dense groundcover for large sites. 'Silver Edge' or 'Gracilis' grows more slowly and has thin oval leaves that are edged with white in summer, turning rosy pink in winter. 'Kewensis' is

Cottage pinks (Dianthus × allwoodii) *form low mats or tufts of grassy blue-green foliage that stays bright and fresh-looking through most of the winter.*

a dwarf form with tiny (only ¼ inch long), rounded, dark green leaves. All adapt to sun or shade and thrive in any well-drained soil. Zone 5.

- *Gaultheria procumbens* / **Wintergreen or checkerberry**

Evergreen. A native woodland plant with fragrant, leathery leaves that are dark green in summer, reddish purple in winter, and bright red berries that last for months. Grows just 3 to 5 inches tall. Spreads slowly and eventually can form a big patch. Sun or shade. Well-drained acid soil. Zone 4.

- *Geranium macrorrhizum* / **Bigroot geranium**

A semi-evergreen perennial with large, soft-textured, musk-scented leaves that turn red-orange in cool weather. Mauve, pink, or white flowers (depending on

cultivar) bloom for a few weeks in early summer on 1-foot stalks. Spreads to form a low patch, 2 to 3 feet wide. Part sun. Well-drained soil. Zone 4. Many other hardy geraniums also have semi-evergreen foliage.

■ *Hedera helix* / **English ivy**

Evergreen. Most cultivars of English ivy, including those with variegated, ruffled, or finely dissected leaves, are hardy to Zone 6. Although the leaves may turn brown and the stems die back in severe winters, new growth appears in late spring. 'Baltica' and 'Thorndale' are two of the hardiest cultivars, usually successful to Zone 5. Both are vigorous vines with medium-sized, lobed, dark green leaves; they can be grown as groundcovers or can climb a wall, fence, or tree. In cold climates, English ivy looks best if grown on the north or east side of a building, where it's shaded from the winter sun and protected from dry west winds. Average soil. It takes a few years for young plants to get established; after that, prune or mow as needed to control their size and spread.

■ *Helleborus* spp. / **Hellebores**

Evergreen or semi-evergreen perennials. Hellebores form clumps or patches of bold, glossy, dark green leaves and bear long-lasting flowers in late winter and early spring. See p. 108 for more information about these plants.

■ *Heuchera* spp. / **Coral bells, heuchera**

Semi-evergreen perennials. Cultivars of *Heuchera × brizoides,* coral bells, form low rosettes of apple green leaves, topped all summer with clouds of tiny coral, rose, pink, or white flowers. 'Palace Purple' and other cultivars of *H. micrantha* form somewhat larger mounds (8 to 12 inches tall) of large, lobed, purple, bronze, silvery, or metallic-looking foliage and have insignificant flowers. All prefer part sun and moist, well-drained soil. Zone 4.

■ *Hypericum calycinum* / **St. John's wort**

Semi-evergreen. A shrubby perennial with neatly spaced pairs of smooth, oval, olive green leaves and bright yellow flowers all summer. Grows 12 to 18 inches tall, spreads 24 inches wide. Sun or shade. Average soil. Zone 5.

Candytuft (Iberis sempervirens) *is a neat, long-lived perennial with bright evergreen foliage, covered with white flowers in early spring.*

■ *Iberis sempervirens* / **Candytuft**

An evergreen perennial that makes tufts or spreading mats, under 1 foot tall and 2 to 3 feet wide, of trailing stems packed with slender dark green leaves. Has clusters of bright white flowers for weeks in spring and sometimes again in fall. Full or part sun. Well-drained soil. Zone 3.

■ *Lamiastrum galeobdolon* / **Yellow archangel**

A semi-evergreen perennial. 'Herman's Pride' and 'Variegata', the two most popular cultivars, both spread to form low patches (under 1 foot tall, 1 to 3 feet wide) of small leaves with jagged edges and silver dots on top. Spikes of bright yellow flowers open in early summer. Sun or shade. Average or moist soil. Zone 4.

■ *Lamium maculatum* / **Spotted dead nettle**

A semi-evergreen perennial with soft, heart-shaped leaves that are green, silver, or two-tone. Trailing stems form a low patch under 8 inches tall, 1 to 3 feet wide.

The leathery fronds of Christmas fern (Polystichum acrostichoides) *stay green all winter, although heavy snow may flatten them to the ground.*

Clusters of pink or white flowers bloom off and on all summer. 'White Nancy' and 'Beacon Silver' are popular cultivars. Sun or shade. Average or moist soil. Zone 4.

- *Pachysandra terminalis* / **Pachysandra or spurge**

An evergreen groundcover with tufts of glossy dark green leaves. Makes a dense carpet, 8 inches tall, under and around trees and shrubs. 'Green Carpet' has especially large and lustrous leaves. 'Variegata' has leaves edged with a thin white stripe. Part or full shade. Average soil. Zone 5.

- *Paxistima* spp. / **Paxistima**

Evergreen. These two native shrubs are dense, bushy, and compact, with small leathery leaves that are bright green in summer, turning darker green, purplish, or bronze in winter. *Paxistima canbyi,* mountain-lover, native to the Alleghenies, grows about 1 foot tall and wide. *P. myrsinites,* Oregon boxwood, native to the western mountains, grows up to 3 feet tall and wide. Sun or part shade. Well-drained soil. Zone 5.

- *Polystichum acrostichoides* / **Christmas fern**

An evergreen fern with rosettes of stiff, leathery, dark green fronds that aren't too lacy. Old fronds flop down on the ground in winter, and new ones arise from the center of the rosette in spring. Grows about 2 feet tall. Part or full shade. Moist, well-drained soil. Zone 3. Try other species of *Polystichum,* too, if you can find them. Most are very attractive, and several are evergreen.

- *Sedum* spp. / **Sedums or stonecrops**

There are scores of sedums sold under many names. Most of the upright, clump-forming types such as 'Autumn Joy' are deciduous, but the low-growing, small-leaved types such as *Sedum acre, S. album,* and *S. spurium* are evergreen or semi-evergreen. Go to your nursery in late fall or early spring to choose sedums for a winter garden. Full or part sun. Well-drained soil. Zone 3.

- *Stachys byzantina* / **Lamb's-ears**

Semi-evergreen perennial. A popular edging plant or groundcover, it forms pros-

trate mats of fuzzy, oblong, silver-gray leaves that can survive several severe frosts but die down by midwinter in cold climates. Bears small lilac flowers on 1-foot spikes in early summer. 'Big Ears', also called 'Helene von Stein', is a vigorous and popular new cultivar with larger than average leaves and few, if any, flowers. Sun or part shade. Average garden soil. Zone 4.

- *Tiarella cordifolia* / **Foamflower**

Evergreen. A woodland wildflower that spreads fast by runners, making low mats of soft-textured, maple-shaped leaves, topped for weeks in spring with dense spikes, 6 to 8 inches tall, of tiny white flowers. Typically has plain green leaves, but there are several new cultivars with reddish or dark veins or markings. *Tiarella wherryi* has similar leaves and pinkish flowers and forms clumps that don't spread. Part or full shade. Moist, well-drained soil. Zone 4.

- *Vaccinium vitis-idaea* / **Mountain cranberry or lingonberry**

Evergreen. A beautiful little shrub with small shiny leaves and tart red berries. The glossy foliage is bright green in summer, garnet red in winter. Spreads by underground runners to form a patch 3 to 6 inches tall and 2 to 3 feet wide. Full or part sun. Rich, moist, well-drained, acid soil. Native to mountain tops; hardy to Zone 2.

- *Vinca minor* / **Myrtle or periwinkle**

Evergreen. A care-free, long-lived groundcover that forms a dense patch of shiny dark green foliage, dotted with round, periwinkle-blue flowers for several weeks in late spring. 'Alba' has green leaves and pure white flowers. 'Sterling Silver' has green-and-cream leaves and lavender-purple flowers. Takes a few years to establish a solid cover, then continues for decades and needs absolutely no care. Grows 4 to 6 inches tall. Sun or shade. Average soil. Zone 4.

- *Waldsteinia ternata* / **Barren strawberry**

An evergreen perennial that spreads fast to form a thick mat of glossy, dark compound leaves, dotted with small yellow flowers in spring. Grows 4 to 6 inches tall, spreads 2 to 3 feet wide. Sun or part shade. Average soil. Zone 4.

In winter, a mixed planting of groundcovers makes a colorful tapestry. The leaves of bearberry (Arctostaphylos uva-ursi), *a low creeping groundcover, turn dark purple-bronze, but lingonberry* (Vaccinium vitis-idaea) *leaves stay bright green. Both plants prefer well-drained, acid soil.*

CHAPTER 2:

TWIGS AND BARK

Winter gives you the opportunity to appreciate some beautiful features of deciduous trees and shrubs that you never notice in summer: the texture of trunk bark, the color of twigs, the size and shape of buds, the geometry of branch patterns. Of course this occurs partly because the leaves are out of the way but also because you see plants in a different light in winter, when the sun sinks so low in the sky that its rays are almost horizontal, illuminating surfaces that are shaded in summer. The sun shines sideways, like the headlights of a car, highlighting vertical items such as tree trunks and penetrating into bushy shrubs. Winter lighting is even more dramatic when the ground is covered with snow, and sunlight is reflected up onto the bottoms of twigs and boughs.

This chapter describes many kinds of trees and shrubs that have such beautiful bark that they would be worth growing for their bark alone. They also, however, provide shade or screening, and some have showy flowers or fruits as well. In choosing ones for your garden, consider how much space you have and how patient you are. Trees such as sycamore *(Platanus occidentalis)* have beautiful bark but grow much too large for most lots. Even small trees such as Japanese tree lilac need an open space at least 15 feet wide to expand their crowns fully. Many

Glossy red twigs make the Siberian dogwood (Cornus alba) *one of the most popular plants for winter gardens.*

shrubs reach 8 to 10 feet tall and wide at maturity, but others remain much smaller or can be pruned to keep them compact.

Typically the bark on tree trunks starts to show its true character when the tree is about ten years old (most trees are a few years old when you buy them) and keeps improving from year to year. Many kinds of birches develop curly, peeling bark. Some cherries have glossy, tight bark. The bark of Chinese dogwood and lacebark elm peels off in irregular flakes to reveal a patchwork of colors. Unlike trees, shrubs usually have their prettiest bark on the youngest twigs. Red-twig dogwoods and shrub willows, for example, will provide a colorful display the first winter after you plant them.

Along with bark and twigs, you notice the shape and structure of trees and shrubs in winter, so it is a good time to plan or do cosmetic pruning. Remove dead, broken, weak, or crossing limbs with a sharp pruning saw or loppers. Study young trees and plan how you will train them as they grow. Any well-kept orchard is a reminder that careful training and pruning transform even common trees with plain gray or tan bark into eye-catching specimens that serve as living sculptures in winter.

SHRUBS WITH DISTINCTIVE TWIGS

All of these shrubs are hardy, adaptable, and fast-growing. Their twigs may have glossy bright-colored bark, papery peeling bark, corky wings, or curling or contorted shapes. You can combine any of these shrubs with conifers, broadleaf evergreens, or grasses for a bed or border that will look lovely all year and outstanding in winter. You could also use a single large shrub such as Harry Lauder's walking stick as a lawn specimen, skirted with a bed of vinca or another evergreen groundcover, or plant a row of red-twig dogwoods or burning bushes for a colorful hedge. If possible, locate these shrubs in a site that gets full sun in winter, since sun highlights the beauty of their twigs.

■ *Cornus* **spp. / Red-twig dogwoods**

DESCRIPTION: These care-free, easy-to-grow shrubs are indispensable for winter color. *Cornus alba,* Siberian dogwood, typically forms an erect clump with bright red twigs. The cultivar 'Sibirica' has especially bright coral red twigs. 'Ele-

'Flaviramea' dogwood (Cornus sericea) *has yellow twigs. Like the red-twig dogwoods, it's a fast-growing, adaptable shrub.*

gantissima' and 'Argenteo-marginata' have variegated green-and-white foliage and red twigs. There are also forms with yellow-variegated leaves or black-red twigs. Zone 3. *C. sanguinea,* blood-twig dogwood, has dark purplish red twigs and tolerates alkaline soil better than the other species. Zone 4. *C. sericea* (formerly *C. stolonifera*), red-osier dogwood, spreads to form a patch, especially in wet soil. It typically has cherry red stems and green leaves. 'Flaviramea' has golden bark. 'Silver and Gold' has gold twigs and white-variegated foliage. Zone 3. Most shrub dogwoods can grow 8 to 10 feet tall and spread much wider than that, but are usually kept small by annual pruning.

CULTURE: Sun, part sun, or shade. These shrubs grow wild in wetlands and are very tolerant of poorly drained soil but thrive in any average garden soil if they are watered during dry spells. Different cultivars are more or less sensitive to leaf-spot diseases during humid weather; infected leaves look ugly and drop early. This can weaken the plants. To minimize the problem, plant in full sun on a site with good air circulation.

All of these shrub dogwoods have the most colorful bark on young shoots. After three or four years, the bark thickens and turns a dull gray. For the best display, cut all the stems flush to the ground every year in midspring, just as the leaf buds start to swell. After a few weeks, new shoots will emerge; they'll grow straight and tall by midsummer and look excellent the next winter. However, this severe pruning means you'll have a bare spot in the garden for a month or so, and you'll never get to see the creamy white flowers and white or blue berries because they only form on second-year growth. As a compromise, you might want to cut only one-half or one-third of the stems every year.

■ *Corylus avellana* 'Contorta' / Harry Lauder's walking stick

DESCRIPTION: This unique shrub has lively, brown-barked shoots that curl and spiral in every direction, and skinny 3-inch catkins dangle from every twig for several weeks in early spring. It makes an excellent centerpiece for a winter garden, growing 6 to 8 feet tall and wide, with large, crisp-textured leaves in summer. Zone 4.

CULTURE: Full sun. Average soil and watering. These plants are usually propagated by grafting, and the understock may sucker repeatedly. Cut any straight shoots back to the base as soon as they appear.

Harry Lauder's walking stick (Corylus avellana *'Contorta') is a large shrub with stems that twist and spiral in all directions. It blooms in late winter and has slender male catkins that dangle in the breeze and tiny, star-shaped female flowers.*

■ *Euonymus alata* / **Burning bush**

DESCRIPTION: Best known for its fluorescent fall foliage, this vigorous, adaptable bush deserves a close look in winter. *Alata* means "wing" and refers to the corky fins that project from the twigs. Some clones have more conspicuous wings than others, so look for this feature when you're buying a plant. Unpruned, burning bush grows up to 10 feet tall and wide, with a graceful vase-shaped profile

and tiers of overlapping branches. 'Compacta' stays smaller, growing to only 6 to 8 feet tall and wide, and has the same attractive profile but thinner twigs. Zone 3.

CULTURE: Sun, part sun, or shade. Adapts to most soils. Can be pruned into formal specimens or hedges but loses its identity; looks best in its natural shape. Trouble-free.

■ *Genista, Cytisus* spp. / Brooms

DESCRIPTION: This is a large group of shrubs that vary in size, habit, flower color, and hardiness. All are bushy plants with masses of parallel, thin, straight, green or gray-green twigs and small, inconspicuous leaves that drop early. Brooms provide a unique winter texture that combines well with needled or broadleaf evergreens. They have showy, pea-like blossoms in spring or summer. Local nurseries may stock only one or two brooms, but several kinds are available by mail. Cultivars of *Genista tinctoria,* which grows 1 to 2 feet tall and 2 to 3 feet wide and has yellow flowers in summer, are hardy to Zone 4. *Cytisus* × *praecox* 'Hollandia' has rosy pink flowers. *C. scoparius* 'Burkwoodii' has garnet red flowers. Both grow 5 to 6 feet tall and are hardy on sheltered sites in Zone 5. Several other brooms are hardy to Zone 6.

CULTURE: Full sun. Brooms need very well-drained soil and make excellent groundcovers or mass plantings for sandy or gravelly banks where little else will grow. Prune once a year, right after they bloom, cutting the stems back by one-third or more. Brooms may freeze to the ground in unusually severe winters; in this case, they don't recover.

■ *Heptocodium miconioides* / Seven son flower

DESCRIPTION: Unknown in American gardens ten years ago, this fast-growing large shrub is now available at many nurseries. The robust stems have shaggy tan and rust-colored bark. It quickly forms a fountain-shaped clump, 10 to 15 feet tall, with large glossy leaves. Blooms in late summer, with small, white, sweet-scented flowers borne in clusters of seven. Zone 5.

CULTURE: Full sun. Average soil. Care-free. Prune older stems to the ground in early spring.

- *Hydrangea* spp. / Hydrangeas

DESCRIPTION: Hydrangea flowers typically dry to a soft beige color and papery texture and hang on long after the leaves drop. Even more distinctive is the cinnamon-colored bark that peels from even young shoots of the climbing or sprawling hydrangea vine, *Hydrangea anomala* subsp. *petiolaris,* or the shrubby, upright-growing oakleaf hydrangea, *H. quercifolia*. Both are hardy to Zone 5. Hydrangea vine grows slowly for a few years, then takes off. It can climb to the top of a tall chimney or tree (it clings tight to masonry or wood but doesn't hurt trees or structures), run along the top of a stone wall or wooden fence, or work as a groundcover on rough ground or rocky banks. It has lacy white flowers in early summer and glossy, heart-shaped leaves. Oakleaf hydrangea forms a multi-stemmed clump, reaching 6 to 8 feet in mild climates but only 3 to 5 feet where cold winters freeze back the tops of the stems. It has cone-shaped flower clusters in early summer and big oaklike leaves that turn wine red in fall.

CULTURE: Sun or shade. Moist but well-drained garden soil. Once established, these hydrangeas are long-lived and trouble-free, and need only routine pruning to remove weak or damaged shoots.

- *Kerria japonica* / Kerria

DESCRIPTION: An old-fashioned, trouble-free shrub with slender, arching stems that have bright green bark. It forms a vase-shaped specimen 4 to 6 feet tall. Golden flowers last a few weeks in midspring. There are single, double, and variegated cultivars. Zone 4.

CULTURE: Part or full shade. Average garden soil. Prune after it flowers, cutting some of the older shoots off at ground level and thinning out any weak or dead wood.

- *Physocarpus opulifolius* / Ninebark

DESCRIPTION: A hardy, adaptable native shrub. The stems have peeling, papery brown bark. Spiraea-like white flowers in spring, reddish seed pods in fall, and green (or yellow in some cultivars) foliage add interest through the year. Typically grows 4 to 6 feet tall. Dwarf cultivars stay 2 to 4 feet tall. Try other ninebark species, too, if you can find them. Zone 3.

'Scarlet Curls' willow (Salix matsudana) *is a fast-growing tree with slender, curly twigs. Willow twigs intensify in color in late winter, as the sun gets brighter and days get longer.*

CULTURE: Full or part sun. Adapts to most soils. Prune once a year, right after it blooms, removing older stems at ground level and cutting out weak or thin shoots. Trouble-free.

■ *Salix* spp. / Willows

DESCRIPTION: Willows are unequaled for variety of twig color and form. Their bark can be charcoal, silver, gold, apricot, salmon, blue-black, blue-purple, or wine red. The twigs can be as slender as spaghetti or as thick as a broomstick. Dozens of species and cultivars are available by mail and sometimes at local nurseries. Here are some of the best: *Salix alba* 'Chermesena' and 'Vitellina' have pencil-sized orange-red and golden yellow twigs, respectively. Zone 3. *S. purpurea* 'Nana' has wiry blue-purple twigs. Zone 4. Willow twigs are typically straight but can be curly. *S. alba* 'Snake' has tan twigs that curl into spirals. Zone 3. *S. matsudana* 'Golden Curls' and 'Scarlet Curls' have yellow or red curly twigs. Zone 5. In each case, the shoots keep their curly shape as they thicken from year to year, but the bark turns gray over time.

CULTURE: Full sun. Average or damp soil. Willows grow very quickly and look best if you prune them frequently and severely. This keeps them compact and healthy and produces the maximum number of young twigs, which have the prettiest bark. You can cut all the stems close to the ground every year in early spring, just as the buds swell; new growth will appear in a month or so. If you wish to avoid making a gap in your garden, cut only one-third to one-half of the stems at a time. If you have an older willow that's grown tall and shabby, cut it off at the ground to renew it. Pruning your willows every spring produces piles of twigs. Root some in water or soil to make new plants, use them for garden stakes, dry them for kindling, or share them with a friend who makes baskets.

TREES WITH BEAUTIFUL BARK

The following deciduous trees all develop attractive bark on their trunks and large limbs as they mature and are small enough to fit into average suburban and city gardens. If you have room to plant only one tree on your list, these are good candidates. Some, such as paperbark maple and parrotia, grow so slowly that it's worth buying the biggest size you can afford. Others, such as birches and aspens,

Paperbark maple (Acer griseum) *is a small, slow-growing tree with cinnamon-colored bark that curls into thin flakes.*

The canoe birch or native white birch (Betula papyrifera) *is traditionally grown in clumps with three or more trunks to show off more of the beautiful bark.*

grow very quickly. Be sure to consider your soil type — lean or fertile, moist or well-drained — when choosing a tree, and get one that's adapted to the site where it will be planted.

Nurseries often start these trees as clumps with two or more trunks. Clump-form trees may cost a little more to start with, but they make beautiful specimens as they mature. The more trunks, the more bark for you to admire. Just be sure that the trunks are spaced well apart where they emerge or that they spread at a wide angle, so that they will not fuse together as they grow.

■ *Acer* spp. / Maples

Acer griseum, paperbark maple, is a small, slow-growing tree with chocolate- or cinnamon-colored bark that peels into thin tight curls. Full sun, average soil. Takes many years to reach 15 feet tall. Zone 5. *A. pensylvanicum,* striped maple or moosewood, has gray bark on its main trunk and twigs with lengthwise green-and-white stripes. Needs part shade and moist, well-drained soil. Zone 4.

■ *Betula* spp. / Birches

Betula papyrifera is the white birch native to New England and the area around the Great Lakes. Where it grows wild, it can also make a good garden plant, but it's subject to fatal insect attacks if stressed by hot, dry summer weather. Most

nurseries now recommend growing the whitespire birch, *B. platyphylla* 'White-spire', instead. A Japanese tree with equally beautiful bark, it's more adaptable to average garden conditions and shows good resistance to bronze birch borers. It's fast-growing, reaching up to 45 feet tall, with a narrow oval crown. Full sun, well-drained soil. Zone 4.

Weeping Trees

Trees with arching or weeping limbs make outstanding specimens in any season, but their graceful silhouette is especially lovely in winter. Although the ones listed here are all deciduous, there are evergreen weeping trees too.

Acer palmatum var. *dissectum*, **laceleaf Japanese maple.**
Forms an umbrella-shaped crown of fine-textured twigs, with lacy leaves in summer. Zone 5.

Betula pendula 'Youngii', **Young's weeping birch.**
Has an erect trunk, white bark, and drooping twigs. Zone 3.

Cornus kousa 'Lustgarten Weeping', **weeping Chinese dogwood.**
A small tree with arching limbs. Forms an umbrella-shaped crown. Zone 5.

Fagus sylvatica 'Pendula', **weeping European beech.**
An impressive tree that eventually becomes quite large, with thick trunk and gnarled limbs. Zone 5.

Malus 'Red Jade' and 'Weeping Candied Apple', **weeping crab apples.**
Small trees with arching limbs that spread wider than tall. Red fruits in winter. Zone 5.

Prunus serrulata 'Pendula', *P. subhirtella* 'Pendula', **weeping flowering cherries.**
Graceful small trees with delicate drooping twigs and masses of flowers in early spring. Zone 5.

Salix alba 'Tristis', **golden weeping willow.**
A large, fast-growing tree with thin twigs that reach down and sweep the ground. Twigs are golden yellow all winter. Zone 5.

River birch (Betula nigra) *has beige or tan bark that peels off in large sheets.*

B. nigra, river birch, is a hardy, healthy native birch with salmon, pinkish beige, or creamy bark that peels off in large sheets. 'Heritage' is a popular cultivar that has especially attractive bark. Both the species and 'Heritage' grow quickly and reach 40 feet or taller. 'Little King' is a slow-growing dwarf cultivar that stays under 10 feet tall for many years and that develops equally beautiful bark. Full sun. All forms of river birch are adapted to damp or poorly drained soil, but they will grow well in average garden soil if watered during dry spells. Zone 4.

■ *Cornus kousa* / Chinese dogwood

This lovely tree is resistant to the anthracnose disease that has killed so many of our native flowering dogwoods in recent years. Along with its large white flowers in early summer and red fruits in fall, it offers multicolored bark for winter interest. Older bark flakes off the trunks and large limbs to make a patchwork of gray, tan, and brown. There are several fine cultivars, including upright, compact, weeping, and variegated forms; most reach 15 to 25 feet tall. All need full or part sun and moist, well-drained soil. Zone 5.

■ *Parrotia persica* / Persian parrotia

A slow-growing tree, usually trained to have multiple trunks and wide-spreading limbs. The gray outer bark flakes off in irregular patches, revealing smooth white inner bark. The deciduous leaves are colorful in both spring and fall and a healthy green all summer. Grows to 15 to 20 feet or taller after many years. Full or part sun; average soil. Zone 4.

■ *Populus tremuloides* / Quaking aspen

Best known for its fluttering leaves that turn bright gold in fall, this small (20- to 40-foot tall) tree also has smooth, thin, tight bark that is pale gray in fall but turns gray-green as the days get longer in late winter and spring. It needs cool, moist soil and does best in the northern or mountain climates where it grows wild. Zone 2. *Populus alba,* white poplar, also has attractive, pale gray-green bark, and its two-tone (dark green on top, white underneath) leaves look dramatic on a windy summer day. It's fast-growing, reaching 20 to 50 feet tall, and adapts to almost any soil. Zone 4.

On mature trees of the Chinese dogwood (Cornus kousa), *the bark forms a colorful patchwork.*

■ *Prunus* spp. / Cherries

Many cherries, including those grown for fruit, have attractive bark; a few are grown primarily for this feature. Even young specimens of *Prunus maackii,* Amur chokecherry, have glossy, curly, caramel-colored bark that glows in the winter sun. This small tree grows 10 to 30 feet tall. Zone 3. *P. sargentii,* Sargent cherry, grows 40 to 50 feet tall and has tight, polished-looking, mahogany-colored bark plus lovely pale pink flowers and colorful fall foliage. Zone 4. *P. serrula,* paperbark cherry, has lovely bark but is not recommended because it's too disease-prone. Amur and Sargent cherry need full sun and rich, moist, well-drained soil.

The lacebark elm (Ulmus parvifolia) *is a neat, disease-resistant elm with beautiful patterns in its bark.*

■ *Stewartia pseudocamellia* / **Japanese stewartia**

Flaky, multicolored bark is just one feature of this fine tree, which also has neat foliage, bright fall colors, and delicate white flowers in summer. It grows 30 to 40 feet tall. Part shade and moist, fertile soil. Zone 5.

■ *Syringa* **spp.** / **Tree lilacs**

Syringa reticulata, Japanese tree lilac, has fragrant, creamy white flowers in June and smooth, cherrylike, reddish brown bark. It grows 20 to 30 feet tall. 'Ivory Silk' is a popular cultivar. *S. pekinensis,* Chinese tree lilac, is a smaller (15- to 20-foot tall) tree with thinner twigs and a daintier appearance, with similar flowers and bark. Both need full sun and well-drained soil. Zone 4.

■ *Ulmus parvifolia* / **Lacebark elm**

This fast-growing, disease-resistant shade tree has neat, healthy foliage and thin bark that flakes off in small patches, making a lacy pattern in shades of green, gray, orange, and brown. Thrives in full sun and rich, moist soil, but tolerates poor soil. Typically grows 30 to 40 feet tall. Zone 5 or 4.

CHAPTER 3:

GRASSES

Ornamental grasses have become very popular in the last decade because they are attractive, inexpensive, easy to grow, and care-free. Grasses combine well with flowering perennials and shrubs. You can add them to perennial beds, mixed borders, foundation plantings, waterside gardens, and meadow- or prairie-type plantings. Their slender leaves and brushy or fluffy seed heads wave gracefully in the slightest breeze and make a soothing, rustling noise. Most grasses turn shades of tan, bronze, and russet after frost, and these soft brownish colors contrast beautifully with green evergreens, red berries, and white snow. Although some grasses turn brittle and break apart in the wind or collapse under the snow, others are surprisingly resilient and look good throughout the winter months. Goldfinches, juncos, sparrows, and other small birds are attracted to clumps of grasses; they eat the seeds and find shelter among the foliage.

The following grasses grow quickly and make impressive clumps in only two or three years after planting. To keep them neat, cut off all the old growth in March, leaving a dense cushion of stubs just a few inches tall. You can divide a big, old clump to make new plants by digging it up in early spring, right after you cut away the old growth, and chopping the rootball into three or more sec-

An erect clump of 'Silver Feather' Japanese silver grass (Miscanthus sinensis) *makes a striking specimen in early winter, with warm beige foliage and fluffy silver seed heads.*

Variegated Japanese sedge (Carex morrowii 'Aureo-variegata') forms evergreen clumps of smooth, slender, striped leaves.

tions. Grass roots are surprisingly tough, so you'll need to use a sharp spade or even an ax to do the division.

- *Calamagrostis* × *acutiflora* / **Feather reed grass**

DESCRIPTION: More reedy than feathery, this grass forms a knee-high clump of slender dark green leaves with hundreds of stiff, skinny flower stalks 5 to 6 feet tall. The foliage grows in cool weather (early spring and late fall), while the flowers and seed heads develop in summer, quickly ripening from green to gold to beige. The flower stalks are strong enough to stand up all winter through wind, rain, and snow. 'Karl Foerster', with plain green leaves, and 'Overdam', with green-and-white striped leaves, are excellent cultivars. Zone 5.

CULTURE: Full or part sun. Not fussy about soil conditions.

The flattened seed heads of northern sea oats (Chasmanthium latifolium) *quiver in the slightest breeze. This grass makes erect clumps that stand up well to winter weather.*

- *Carex morrowii* 'Aureo-variegata' / **Variegated Japanese sedge**

DESCRIPTION: This grasslike perennial forms a low, swirling tuft (12 inches tall, 18 inches wide) of slender, glossy, evergreen leaves striped lengthwise with green and yellow. Zone 6 or 5.

CULTURE: Part sun. Prefers moist, fertile soil but adapts to average conditions.

- *Chasmanthium latifolium* / **Northern sea oats**

DESCRIPTION: This adaptable, care-free grass forms a clump 3 to 4 feet tall. Leaves that are rather short and wide for a grass clothe the bottom half of each stalk, and clusters of flat seed heads dangle above. The leaves and seed heads turn from green to warm brown in the fall, then gradually fade to beige. They hold up well into the winter. Zone 4.

CULTURE: Sun, part sun, or shade. (This is one of the best grasses for a shady site.) Average soil. Tolerates wet or dry conditions. Often self-seeds. Look for seedlings in spring and pull them out or transplant them.

■ *Deschampsia caespitosa* / **Tufted hair grass**

DESCRIPTION: Attractive all year, this grass forms a mound of foliage about 2 feet tall and wide that stays green well into the winter even in northern climates, remaining evergreen in mild winters. In summer, it makes a cloud of fluffy flower heads in shades of green, yellow, or purple. Zone 4.

CULTURE: Part shade. Prefers well-drained but evenly moist soil. Trim off the flower stalks in late summer; they break down and don't last into the winter.

■ *Erianthus ravennae* / **Ravenna grass**

DESCRIPTION: A giant grass that needs plenty of space but makes a wonderful specimen. Its broad, arching leaves form a mound up to 6 feet tall and wide, and fluffy seed heads on stiff stalks reach 10 to 12 feet tall. Rich green in summer, the whole plant turns tan in winter, and stands up well to wind and snow. Zone 4.

CULTURE: Full sun. Average or dry soil.

■ *Festuca ovina* var. *glauca* / **Blue fescue**

DESCRIPTION: This grass has very fine-textured leaves and forms a neat, dense, pincushion-like clump about 1 foot tall and wide. Named cultivars such as 'Sea Urchin' have especially nice foliage, in lovely shades of blue that combine well with other plants. Slender flower spikes appear in summer and quickly ripen from blue to tan. Zone 4.

Blue oat grass, *Helictotrichon sempervirens,* looks and grows like blue fescue grass, but it forms larger clumps, has longer, wider leaves, and blooms sparsely, if at all. Zone 4.

CULTURE: Full sun. Well-drained soil. Blue fescue is a cool season grass and looks best if you trim it flush to the ground twice a year. Cut it down in August, and the new foliage that grows in fall will stay fresh until it's flattened by heavy snow. Cut it again as soon as the snow melts in late winter, because blue fescue is one of the first plants to start growing in spring.

Blue fescue grass (Festuca ovina *var.* glauca) *forms dense, compact clumps of very fine-textured leaves. It grows best in the cool weather of fall and spring.*

- *Liriope* spp. / Lilyturf

DESCRIPTION: Creeping lilyturf, *Liriope spicata,* spreads to form a mat of grassy-looking foliage and bears spikes of small, pale purple flowers in late summer. It stays under 1 foot tall and makes a good groundcover under and around trees and shrubs. It can also substitute for grass on shady or sloping sites. Zone 5 or 4. Regular lilyturf, *L. muscari,* forms clumps, rather than spreading, and has more showy flowers and larger leaves that can be plain green or striped with gold or white. It grows about 18 inches tall and can be used as a specimen, groundcover, or edging. Zone 6 or 5. Both creeping and regular lilyturf stay green and fresh-looking until the temperature drops to around zero; then they freeze to the ground. New growth appears in late spring.

CULTURE: Part sun or shade. Grows best with regular watering in well-drained soil but tolerates short dry spells.

- *Miscanthus sinensis* / Japanese silver grass

DESCRIPTION: Cultivars of this grass are among the most popular ornamental grasses. All form large vase-shaped clumps of long arching leaves and bear fluffy seed heads in fall. They stand up partway through dry winters, but the clumps tend to splay apart, tip over, or break down in heavy snow or ice storms. Most cultivars grow 4 to 6 feet tall and are hardy to Zone 5.

CULTURE: Full sun. Average or moist soil.

- *Panicum virgatum* / Switch grass

DESCRIPTION: An adaptable native grass that stands up well to winter storms. It forms a clump 4 to 5 feet tall and 2 to 3 feet wide, with masses of fine-textured, branched seed heads held above a mound of arching leaves. Regular switch grass has leaves that are green in summer, tan in fall and winter. 'Rotstrahlbusch' develops good red fall color before turning tan. 'Heavy Metal' is an unusual blue-gray color in summer and turns tan in winter. Zone 4.

CULTURE: Full or part sun. Average or poor soil. Water it during long dry spells.

- *Schizachyrium scoparium* / Little bluestem

DESCRIPTION: One of the best grasses for winter color, with curly leaves that turn a warm cinnamon brown, sometimes tinged with orange or purple. It forms

Perennials with Interesting Stalks and Pods

Like grasses, many perennials have stiff stalks and conspicuous pods or seed heads that add height and interest to a winter landscape. The following remain attractive well into the winter and may last until spring if they aren't knocked down by severe storms.

Asclepias tuberosa, butterfly weed
Baptisia australis, false indigo
Echinacea purpurea, purple coneflower
Hibiscus spp., mallows
Iris sibirica, Siberian iris
Linum perenne, perennial flax
Perovskia atriplicifolia, Russian sage
Sedum 'Autumn Joy', sedum

Dried stalks of grasses and perennials such as Sedum *'Autumn Joy' add color and texture to a garden throughout the winter and provide shelter and seeds for the birds.*

Little bluestem (Schizachyrium scoparium) *turns russet in fall; the clumps stand up until spring.*

erect clumps 2 to 3 feet tall. The tops of the stalks are dotted with tiny, fluffy seed heads that sparkle in the sun. Rain or snow may knock it down, but it stands right up again and looks good until spring. Zone 3.

CULTURE: Full or part sun. Average or poor soil. Tolerates dry spells.

■ *Sporobolus heterolepsis* / **Prairie dropseed**

DESCRIPTION: A lovely grass that forms a graceful, arching mound, about 2 feet wide, of very slender leaves that turn warm gold or honey-colored in fall and winter. Delicate, fragrant flowers appear in late summer. Zone 3.

CULTURE: Full or part sun. Average or poor soil; tolerates damp or dry sites.

Chapter 4:
Winter Fruits and Berries

Many kinds of trees, shrubs, and vines produce brightly colored berries or small fruits as a way of attracting birds, who disseminate the seeds. This system offers a double bonus to gardeners. You can enjoy looking at the berries, and then you can watch the birds who come to eat them.

As you watch the birds who come to your garden, you'll notice that they're alert and curious, and that they're choosy eaters. They fly from tree to tree and bush to bush, exploring and nibbling. Birds gobble some fruits, such as honeysuckle and dogwood berries, as soon as they ripen in late summer or early fall, but leave others, such as pyracantha berries and crab apples, until late winter or spring. If you have room to plant a variety of fruit-bearing shrubs and trees, you can attract birds to your garden over a long season. If you have room for only one or two of these plants, you might want to choose one with berries that the birds shun until spring so that you can enjoy the berries in winter. You can always fill a feeder with seeds to attract birds in the meantime.

*Hybrid crab apples (*Malus *cultivars) produce colorful but tough fruits that hang on the limbs all winter. In spring, after repeated freezing and thawing has made the fruits soft and mushy, robins and other birds flock to eat them.*

Most berries are bright red or orange, but some are gold, pink, white, blue, black, or gray. They all look cheerful on a winter day, perhaps sparkling in the sun against a background of dark evergreens, or highlighted with a dusting of snow or a coating of ice. Except where noted, the plants listed below are all deciduous. Most start producing berries or fruits when they are young — often the first year you plant them — and bear regularly year after year.

■ *Aronia arbutifolia* / Chokeberry

DESCRIPTION: Clusters of small bright red berries dangle from every twig of this erect, thicket-forming, native shrub. Birds shun them, preferring other fruits, so the display lasts all winter. 'Brilliantissima' is a popular cultivar, 6 to 10 feet tall, with especially bright red fall foliage and small white flowers in spring. Although it's harder to find at nurseries, *Aronia melanocarpa*, black chokeberry, has larger, purple-black berries that do attract birds. It also has larger, prettier flowers and a more compact, rounded shape. It grows 4 to 6 feet tall. Zone 4.

CULTURE: Full or part sun. Both species are native to wetlands and tolerate poorly drained soil, but they thrive in average soil too. Chokeberries are easy to grow and care-free, ideal for shrub borders or semiwild gardens.

■ *Berberis thunbergii* / Japanese barberry

DESCRIPTION: Tiny red berries dangle like earrings from the wickedly spiny twigs of Japanese barberry throughout the fall and early winter. This shrub is often used for sheared hedges; unpruned, it forms a dense, broad, arching mound at least 6 feet tall and wide. New compact cultivars such as 'Crimson Pygmy' stay small (under 2 feet tall, spreading somewhat wider than that) and don't need pruning. Both full-size and dwarf cultivars are available with bright green, golden yellow, or dark reddish purple foliage. They're among the first shrubs to leaf out in spring and they all turn bright red in fall. Zone 4. Wintergreen barberry, *Berberis julianae,* and warty barberry, *B. verruculosa,* are large, rounded shrubs at least 6 feet tall and wide, with shiny navy blue berries and sharp-toothed evergreen leaves that are glossy green in summer and maroon in winter. Zone 6.

CULTURE: This adaptable shrub grows in sun or shade but needs full sun for maximum fruiting and best foliage color. Any well-drained soil is fine. Prune if and when you choose. Needs no other care.

Red chokeberry (Aronia arbutifolia) *is a care-free, adaptable native shrub with small red berries that last all winter.*

Bright red berries dangle like earrings from the spiny twigs of Japanese barberry (Berberis thunbergii).

- *Callicarpa* spp. / Beautyberries

DESCRIPTION: Although the berries don't last until spring, a beautyberry bush is a spectacular sight in fall and early winter, with tight clusters of tiny lilac-purple or white berries dotting every stem like beads on a string. Nurseries offer a few species and cultivars, all desirable. Most kinds grow about 4 feet tall, with arching stems. Zone 6 or 5.

CULTURE: Full or part sun. Prefers moist, loamy, well-drained soil. Fruits best if you grow three or more of the same kind together, spaced about 3 feet apart. Prune hard in early spring, cutting last year's stems down to the ground. This keeps the plant bushy. Berries form on new wood.

- *Celastrus* spp. / Bittersweets

DESCRIPTION: These vigorous woody vines bear an unforgettable display of red-orange berries, revealed in fall when the leaves turn gold and drop, and persisting through winter until eaten by birds. Beware of *Celastrus orbiculatus,* Oriental bittersweet. Although it's commonly sold, it is too vigorous for most sites; it's considered a serious weed in parts of New England. *C. scandens,* American bittersweet, is more desirable because it is less aggressive, but it still needs watching. It's also hardier, to Zone 3.

CULTURE: Full or part sun. Average soil. Separate male and female plants are needed to set fruit. Train them on a sturdy trellis or along the top of a fence, don't let them climb into a tree, and prune severely to keep them under control. Fruiting begins a few years after planting.

- *Clematis* spp. / Clematis

DESCRIPTION: These vines are best known for their prolific floral display, but some kinds (especially the species, not hybrid cultivars) look equally impressive in the fall and winter, when each flower is replaced with a fluffy, silvery seed head 1 to 3 inches wide. The following three species have especially attractive and long-lasting seed heads. *Clematis macropetala,* downy clematis, blooms in early summer with nodding blue-violet flowers. (There are white, pink, and double-flowered cultivars, too.) It grows 6 to 10 feet tall. *C. tangutica,* golden clematis, has dangling, bell-shaped, yellow flowers and grows 8 to 10 feet tall. *C. terniflora,* sweet autumn clematis, has masses of fragrant, starry white flowers and grows to 20 feet or taller. All are hardy to Zone 4.

CULTURE: Full sun. Average soil. Train the vine up a wire fence, trellis, twiggy shrub, or a piece of netting stretched against a board or brick fence or wall. Prune downy clematis right after it blooms, cutting it back partway. Prune golden clematis and sweet autumn clematis in late winter, cutting all the stems back to within 1 foot of the ground.

■ *Cotoneaster* spp. / Cotoneasters

DESCRIPTION: The many kinds of cotoneasters vary in habit, from creeping or trailing groundcovers, to low mounded shrubs, to large bushes with arching stems. Most have red or reddish berries borne singly or clustered along the stems in fall and small pink or white flowers in spring. Deciduous species may have bright fall foliage. Evergreen species typically have neat little leaves that turn purple or bronze in cold weather.

Ask a local nursery or other gardeners for advice when choosing a cotoneaster that will be hardy, healthy, and the right size and shape for your site. *Cotoneaster adpressus* 'Praecox', early cotoneaster; *C. apiculatus,* cranberry cotoneaster; *C. dammeri,* bearberry cotoneaster; *C. horizontalis,* rockspray cotoneaster; and *C. salicifolius* 'Scarlet Leader' are good low-growing types that reach 1 to 3 feet tall and 2 to 6 feet wide. *C. divaricatus,* spreading cotoneaster, is a loosely rounded shrub that grows up to 6 feet tall and 12 feet wide. *C. multiflorus,* many-flowered cotoneaster, grows up to 10 feet tall and 15 feet wide and makes an impressive fountain-like specimen for large gardens. In general, evergreen cotoneasters are hardy to Zone 6, and deciduous ones are hardy to Zone 4.

CULTURE: Full or part sun. Fertile, moist, well-drained soil. Cotoneasters are subject to fire blight and other diseases, but under good growing conditions they are beautiful shrubs with year-round appeal.

■ *Crataegus* spp. / Hawthorns

DESCRIPTION: Two kinds of hawthorn make especially good trees for small gardens. Both have clusters of dull white flowers (with a fetid scent, unfortunately) in late spring, healthy foliage that turns red in fall, clusters of red-orange berries that last into the winter, and attractive gray bark. *Crataegus phaenopyrum,*

Most hollies have red berries, but 'Xanthocarpa' is a cultivar of American holly (Ilex opaca) with golden berries that look bright and cheerful even on dark winter days.

Washington hawthorn, grows 20 to 25 feet tall, usually with multiple trunks and an oval crown that's a dense tangle of extremely thorny twigs; birds find safety inside and often nest in these trees. Zone 3. *C. viridis* 'Winter King' grows about 25 feet tall, usually with a single trunk and vase-shaped crown, and has few thorns. Zone 4.

CULTURE: Full or part sun. Hawthorns adapt to any well-drained soil, need only routine pruning, and are generally trouble-free.

■ *Ilex decidua, I. verticillata* / **Possum haw, winterberry holly**

DESCRIPTION: Although deciduous, these native hollies are among the most impressive plants for a winter garden, because their pea-sized scarlet berries are so abundant and so colorful. How long the berries last varies from year to year, depending on how hungry the birds are. Some years they're gone by Thanksgiving; other years they remain until spring. *Ilex decidua,* possum haw, grows fairly quickly, reaches 15 feet or taller, and can be pruned into a small tree. Zone 5. *I. verticillata,* winterberry holly, grows more slowly, spreads by suckers, and forms a twiggy thicket up to 10 feet tall and wide. Zone 4. There are many fine cultivars of each species, differing in berry color (some are more orange than red, and there are even yellow-fruited forms) and mature size and habit (rounded or erect).

CULTURE: Both possum haw and winterberry holly tolerate part or full shade but produce many more berries when grown in full sun. They grow wild in wetlands but adapt well to average garden soil. Hollies produce male and female flowers on separate plants, so ask the nursery to recommend a suitable male for whichever female cultivar(s) you choose. The sexes don't have to be planted side by side, since bees will carry the pollen several hundred feet. You can display the female(s) in a prominent place and use the male to fill a gap elsewhere on your property.

■ *Ilex* spp. / Evergreen hollies

'Blue Princess', 'China Girl', 'Old Heavy Berry', and other female evergreen hollies produce bright red (or sometimes yellow) berries that stand out against their dark winter foliage. For more about these plants, see pp. 28–29.

■ *Malus* spp. / Hybrid crab apples

DESCRIPTION: Modern crab apples are small trees, 15 to 25 feet tall, with white, pink, or rosy flowers in spring and small, hard red, purple, or golden fruits that ripen in early fall. The fruits remain colorful and decorative through the winter but gradually turn mushy. When the fruits are soft enough, flocks of waxwings, robins, and other birds gather in the trees to eat them. There are so many good crab apple cultivars that it's hard to choose. Consider flower color, fruit color, foliage color (green or reddish purple), and mature tree size and shape (the crown can be oval, vase-shaped, round, or weeping). Zone 4.

CULTURE: Full sun. Well-drained garden soil. Prune routinely in late winter to establish the shape, encourage wide branch angles, eliminate weak or crossing limbs, and remove suckers. Most old-fashioned crab apples were susceptible to

Tight clusters of bright red berries line the twigs of winterberry holly (Ilex verticillata), *a native shrub that's very adaptable and easy to grow.*

Crab apples, native to the north temperate zone, have bright fruits that last for months — sometimes until the flowers bloom in spring.

scab, rust, and powdery mildew, which made the leaves look ugly and drop early. Some modern cultivars have much better disease resistance, so ask about this when you're choosing which one to plant.

■ *Myrica pensylvanica* / **Bayberry**

DESCRIPTION: Native along the eastern seaboard and well adapted to inland gardens, bayberry is a vigorous, care-free shrub with glossy leaves that turn dark maroon or bronze in fall and cling until early winter. When the leaves finally drop, you see that the twigs of the female plants are totally crusted with tight clusters of tiny, waxy, blue-gray berries. Both leaves and berries have a spicy aroma. Bayberry can be sheared or pruned, or you can let it spread naturally into an irregular, mounded shrub, typically 4 to 8 feet tall and 6 to 10 feet wide. Zone 2.

CULTURE: Sun or shade. Adapts to almost any soil, wet or dry. Prune in spring, if desired. Spreads by suckers; cut them off or pull them out if they reach too far. Trouble-free.

- *Pyracantha* spp. / Pyracantha, firethorn

DESCRIPTION: Pyracanthas have long been popular in mild-winter climates. Now there are some new hybrids that do well in Zone 6 and on sheltered sites in Zone 5. These are all dense, thorny shrubs with semi-evergreen foliage, white flowers in spring, and clusters of berries that last all winter. 'Apache' has unusually long-lasting bright red berries and a compact, spreading habit; it grows to 4 to 5 feet tall. 'Gnome' has orange berries and is compact and rounded, remaining under 6 feet tall. 'Mohave' has orange-red berries and an erect, angular shape, reaching up to 10 feet tall. 'Teton' has golden yellow berries and a narrow, upright habit, reaching 12 feet tall by 4 feet wide.

CULTURE: Full or part sun. Any well-drained soil. Prune in early spring, removing dead or damaged wood and shaping the bush as you choose. Can be espaliered against a wall or building for extra shelter from cold and wind, and an espaliered specimen makes a wonderful focal point for a winter garden. Unlike old-fashioned pyracanthas, the new cultivars have good resistance to scab, fire blight, and other diseases.

- *Rosa* spp. / Roses

DESCRIPTION: Many kinds of shrub or "landscape" roses, both old-fashioned and modern, produce edible, bright red-orange "hips" or fruits that last well into the winter. (Of course, the hips can develop only if you let the flowers fade naturally and don't prune them off.) Cultivars and hybrids of the rugosa rose, *Rosa rugosa,* bear hips the size of cherry tomatoes. Rugosa-type roses have unusually healthy foliage and large magenta, pink, or white flowers, and form rounded bushes 3 to 6 feet tall and wide. Zone 4. *R. eglanteria,* sweetbriar rose, has long prickly canes, clear pink single flowers, and masses of small red fruits. It grows to 8 feet tall and wide. Zone 3. *R. rubrifolia,* red-leaf rose, bears small bright

The bright red hips or fruits of the sweetbriar rose (Rosa eglanteria) *ripen in late fall and last through the winter, providing food for birds and wildlife.*

red hips on arching, almost thornless canes that have distinctive reddish purple bark. It looks beautiful against the snow. Zone 4.

CULTURE: Full sun. Rugosa roses thrive in any well-drained garden soil and are the best roses for dry, sandy sites. By contrast, Virginia rose and red-leaf rose are among the only roses tolerant of poorly drained soil; they also thrive in average or dry soil. These are all care-free, disease-resistant shrubs. Prune them in early spring, just as the buds start to swell, removing old, weak, or damaged shoots at ground level and cutting back vigorous shoots to stimulate branching.

Invasive Plants

Invasive plants, often simply called weeds, are plants that germinate and grow quickly with no help from a gardener and are hard to remove or control. Many kinds of berry-producing plants, whose seeds are spread by birds, become invasive in moist woodlands, along roadsides, and in abandoned farm fields in the eastern United States. This group includes red chokeberry, Oriental bittersweet, Japanese barberry, multiflora rose *(Rosa multiflora),* and several kinds of honeysuckle (*Lonicera* spp.) and privet (*Ligustrum* spp.). A plant that's invasive in one region, however, may be hard to grow someplace else. The best thing to do is check with local experts and avoid planting any berrying plant that's considered invasive in your region. That way you won't cause problems for yourself or your neighborhood.

*Sumacs (*Rhus *spp.) produce bright red berrylike fruits that are an important source of winter food for dozens of bird species, but these shrubs spread rapidly by suckers and by seeds, so some gardeners consider them weedy.*

Berry-Eating Birds

Keep a pair of binoculars and a field guide near the window so you can watch and identify the birds that come to your garden. You might see berry-eating birds such as robins, bluebirds, catbirds, mockingbirds, bluejays, cedar waxwings, thrushes, vireos, thrashers, woodpeckers, chickadees, doves, quail, pheasants, grouse, blackbirds, starlings, and crows. Sparrows, finches, juncos, cardinals, doves, quail, chickadees, nuthatches, titmice, and other birds eat the small dry seeds produced by grasses, perennial wildflowers, and weeds, and by trees such as pines, spruces, and birches.

A songbird like this female cardinal eats dozens of berries and seeds on a cold winter day.

■ *Symphoricarpos* spp. / Snowberry, Indian currant, coralberry

DESCRIPTION: *Symphoricarpos albus,* white snowberry, is one of the few hardy shrubs with white berries; marble-sized, they show up well against a background of dark evergreens. *S. orbiculatus,* Indian currant, has smaller, reddish purple berries. Both are open, upright shrubs 3 to 6 feet tall, hardy to Zone 3. *S.* × *chenaultii* 'Hancock', coralberry, is a low, spreading shrub, under 2 feet tall and 6 feet wide, that makes a good large-scale groundcover. It has rose-pink berries and is hardy to Zone 5. Although the berries don't last past midwinter, these care-free shrubs bear abundant crops year after year.

CULTURE: Sun or shade. These adaptable shrubs grow in any well-drained soil. Prune every year in early spring, removing old stems and unwanted suckers to ground level and cutting the other stems back partway to induce branching.

■ *Viburnum* spp. / Viburnums, cranberrybushes, highbush cranberries

DESCRIPTION: Viburnums are small to large shrubs, deciduous or evergreen. Most kinds produce berries that ripen in summer or fall and stay on the bush for weeks or months, depending on how hungry the birds are. The two species with the least appetizing and thus the longest-lasting berries are the European cranberrybush, *Viburnum opulus,* and American cranberrybush, *V. trilobum.* Both are upright, open shrubs 10 to 12 feet tall, with maplelike leaves that develop good fall color, lacy clusters of white flowers in spring, and soft red berries the size of raisins. These berries are translucent and gleam on a sunny winter day. Mail-order nurseries list cultivars with compact growth habits, yellow fruits, or larger than average red fruits. Zone 4 or 3.

CULTURE: Full or part sun. Fertile, moist soil. Water regularly during summer dry spells. Subject to aphids, which distort the new growth but cause no serious harm. Prune by cutting old and weak stems to the ground in early spring.

Chapter 5:
First Flowers

April is a difficult month for gardeners in cold climates. The calendar says it's spring, and indeed the sun is getting brighter and the days are getting longer. In many years, however, there's still snow on the ground in early April. There might even be a flurry or two late in the month, and frosts can continue through May. Despite the lingering cold, though, gardeners start examining their plants, hoping to find swollen buds and craving the sight of fresh flowers.

Most people celebrate bright yellow forsythia and daffodils as the first signs of spring, without realizing that witch hazel, Cornelian cherry dogwood, hellebores, snowdrops, and several other plants start blooming as much as a month earlier. Although not quite as showy as the flowers that follow, these extra-early bloomers are beautiful if you see them up close, and they promise that winter is almost over. Whether you call it late winter or early spring, the time when these earliest flowers appear is a season of hope.

When each kind of plant starts blooming varies considerably from place to place. Serviceberry trees flower in April in Cincinnati but wait until May in Minneapolis. Crocuses bloom in city parks a week earlier than they do out in the

Winter aconite (Eranthus hyemalis) *is a diminutive charmer, with buttercup yellow flowers on a ruff of leaves. On a suitable site, it spreads by seed to form large patches.*

suburbs. Even on a single lot, timing of bloom depends on exposure. For the earliest flowers, choose a site that's warmed by the sun and sheltered from cold winds, against a south-facing wall, fence, or hedge or on a south-facing slope. Watch your property as the snow melts in spring, and plant early bloomers in those places where the snow melts soonest, not where it lingers.

Choosing sheltered sites is especially effective for forcing bulbs and perennials into early bloom. The flowers on some of these low-growing plants are surprisingly tough. Their petals can be covered with ice, frost, or snow and remain unblemished after it melts. Shrubs and trees are less reliable. There's a risk that they may bloom too early on a sheltered site, and in some years their buds or blossoms may get killed by a late frost. Still, many gardeners accept that risk in return for a stunning early display in other years.

POPULAR LANDSCAPE TREES AND SHRUBS

These plants all have showy, colorful flowers in early spring. They are all readily available from good local nurseries in the regions where they grow well. When choosing a spring-blooming tree or shrub, consider its cold-hardiness, soil preference, ultimate size, and rate of growth, as well as its flowers.

- *Acer rubrum* / Red maple

    DESCRIPTION: A fast-growing shade tree with dangling clusters of red flowers that appear in very early spring. It also has colorful fall foliage, and on some trees the new twigs turn red in winter. Grows to 40 feet or taller. Zone 4.

    CULTURE: Full sun. Native to wet sites throughout the eastern United States. Adapts well to average garden soil. Makes a good shade tree for lawns.

- *Amelanchier laevis* / Serviceberry, shadbush

    DESCRIPTION: Small white or pale pink flowers line the limbs of this small native tree in early spring. It's often grown with multiple trunks to show off its handsome bark. Neat leaves turn bright colors in fall. Grows 15 to 25 feet tall. Zone 4. Related species are also early bloomers and make fine garden specimens.

    CULTURE: Full or part sun. Prefers moist, well-drained, acidic soil. A healthy and care-free tree.

*Flowering quince (*Chaenomeles *cultivars) bear pink, scarlet, orange, or white flowers in early spring. Training the stems against a wall or building encourages early blooming and protects the flowers from late frosts.*

■ *Chaenomeles* spp. / Flowering quince

DESCRIPTION: A tough, adaptable shrub with almost fluorescent pink, scarlet, orange (or sometimes white) flowers that resemble apple blossoms. Cultivars differ in flower color and habit. Most are dense bushy or upright shrubs, 4 to 8 feet tall, with crooked, thorny twigs. Deciduous. Zone 4.

CULTURE: Full or part sun. Average garden soil. Can be pruned as a hedge or trained as an espalier. May drop its leaves early some years due to drought or disease but recovers the next season.

Some years, heaths (Erica carnea) *are already blooming when the snow melts, and their tiny, bell-shaped pink or white flowers last for several weeks.*

■ *Cornus mas* / **Cornelian cherry dogwood**

DESCRIPTION: A small tree or large shrub with clusters of small greenish yellow flowers. The flowers are smaller than forsythia blossoms but open a few weeks earlier. Cherry-sized red berries in summer, glossy foliage with rich fall colors, and flaking bark add interest the rest of the year. Grows to 15 feet or taller, with a single or multiple trunks. Highly recommended for its beauty and adaptability. Zone 4. Several nurseries are starting to offer *Cornus officinalis,* Japanese cornelian cherry dogwood, a similar but somewhat larger tree that blooms even earlier and has more showy bark. Zone 4.

CULTURE: Full or part sun. Average soil. Once established, tolerates moderate droughts. Much more adaptable and trouble-free than the common flowering dogwood *(C. florida).*

■ *Erica* spp. / Heaths

DESCRIPTION: These small evergreen shrubs make an excellent groundcover for sandy or acidic soils. They form a low mat of dark, needlelike foliage and bear clusters of small, bell-shaped rose, pink, or white flowers. They can start blooming even before the snow melts and continue for many weeks. *Erica carnea* 'Springwood White' and 'Springwood Pink' are two of the best and most popular cultivars. Specialty nurseries offer many other heaths; if your soil conditions are right, these plants are an excellent investment. Zone 5 or 4.

CULTURE: Full or part sun. Heaths need well-drained soil, preferably acidic or neutral. On a suitable site, heaths live for decades and require little care. Just shear them back halfway after they bloom to keep them tidy and promote dense, vigorous new growth.

■ *Forsythia* spp. / Forsythia

DESCRIPTION: There are many kinds of forsythias; all are deciduous shrubs with slender twigs and yellow flowers. Although they are very showy and very popular, common forsythias are unreliable north of Zone 6, since the buds freeze in severe winters. For better results, choose one of the following new cultivars, which were bred especially for their hardiness. *Forsythia* × *intermedia* 'Meadowlark' reaches 10 feet tall and wide and has bright yellow flowers. *F. ovata* 'Northern Sun' grows to 8 feet, bearing medium yellow flowers. *F. mandschurica* 'Vermont Sun' gets to 6 to 8 feet tall and wide; its lemon yellow flowers bloom about a week earlier than other kinds. All bloom abundantly even in Zone 4.

CULTURE: Full sun. Average garden soil. Prune after flowering to control size and shape, removing some of the oldest shoots at ground level. Don't be surprised to find a few forsythia blossoms in late fall; plenty more will follow in spring.

■ *Hamamelis* spp. / Witch hazels

DESCRIPTION: These large shrubs or small trees have sweet-scented, spidery yellow, gold, or reddish flowers and attractive deciduous leaves. They are often the first shrubs to bloom, preceding forsythias by a month or more. Their flowers last for weeks, as the petals unfurl on mild days and curl up again when the temperature drops. Vernal or Ozark witch hazel, *Hamamelis vernalis,* is the hardiest species (Zone 4). It's shrubby, under 10 feet tall, and may spread by suckers

'Arnold Promise' witch hazel (Hamamelis × intermedia) *is one of the first trees to bloom in late winter, and its golden yellow flowers have a sweet, penetrating aroma.*

to form a patch. Chinese witch hazel, *H. mollis,* and hybrid witch hazels, *H. × intermedia,* grow into vase-shaped trees 15 to 20 feet tall and are hardy to Zone 6 or protected sites in Zone 5.

CULTURE: Full or part sun. Chinese and hybrid witch hazels prefer moist, well-drained soil. Vernal witch hazel is quite adaptable and grows well on wet, average, or dry sites. Prune in early summer if you need to shape young plants. Established plants are care-free.

■ *Magnolia* **spp. / Magnolias**

DESCRIPTION: Most hardy magnolias are deciduous trees or shrubs with large white, cream, pink, or rosy purple flowers that open just before the leaves expand. In good years, a flowering magnolia is a beautiful cloud of bloom, but a late hard

'Dr. Merrill' magnolia (Magnolia × loebneri) *grows quickly into an upright,
medium-sized tree and blooms abundantly year after year, bearing large white flowers
with a mild, pleasant fragrance.*

frost can turn the blossoms into brown mush overnight. Most gardeners will risk the occasional disappointment for the intervening years of beauty. *Magnolia* × *loebneri* 'Dr. Merrill' is often the first to bloom, with fragrant, starry, white flowers. It's a fast-growing tree that reaches 30 feet tall. 'Leonard Messel' is similar but has pink flowers. Zone 5. *M. stellata,* star magnolia, has starry white flowers and blooms a week or two later than 'Dr. Merrill'. It grows more slowly and forms a broader, rounded shrub or tree 10 to 20 feet tall. 'Centennial' and 'Royal Star' are good cultivars. Zone 4. Cultivars of *M. soulangiana,* saucer magnolia, bloom even later. These trees form spectacular specimens up to 30 feet tall and have large, upright, goblet-shaped flowers with thick, waxy, white or purplish petals. Zone 5. All magnolias start blooming at an early age.

CULTURE: Full or part sun. Deep, well-drained, fertile, moist soil. Water regularly during droughts. Use mulch or groundcover to cover the soil under a magnolia; don't try to maintain a lawn or plant flowers there. Magnolias need little pruning; simply remove dead or damaged shoots. Once established, they are healthy, care-free, and long-lived.

■ *Prunus* **spp. / Flowering cherries**

DESCRIPTION: Valued first for their flowers, these small trees or large shrubs also have attractive bark and twigs, and those listed here also have colorful fall foliage. Most cherries bloom abundantly but briefly, but the hybrids 'Hally Jolivette' (soft pink flower; 15 to 20 feet tall) and 'Okame' (purplish pink flowers; 25 feet tall) have a longer than average blooming season, lasting for a few weeks in early spring. *Prunus subhirtella* var. *autumnalis* (soft pink flowers in spring and again in fall, erect form, 20 to 40 feet tall) and its cultivars 'Snow Goose' (white flowers, upright form, 20 feet tall), 'Pendula' (pink flowers, weeping limbs, 20 feet tall), and 'Snow Fountains' (white flowers, weeping limbs, 20 feet tall) also have long-lasting flowers. All of these cherries are hardy in Zone 5, although extreme cold may damage the buds or blossoms in some years.

CULTURE: Full sun. Deep, fertile, well-drained soil. Water during summer dry spells. Prune as needed to thin the crown and eliminate narrow crotches. Under favorable conditions, cherries are fast-growing trees. The cultivars listed above have healthy, disease-resistant foliage, but they may be attacked by borers or other insect pests.

'PJM' rhododendron (Rhododendron) *is one of the first shrubs to bloom in spring, with masses of bright magenta flowers. It also has neat, small, evergreen leaves that turn rich purple-bronze in winter.*

■ *Rhododendron* spp. / Rhododendrons

DESCRIPTION: The earliest rhododendrons bloom before or along with forsythias. Some of the hardiest and most widely available are 'Pink Diamond', also called 'Weston's Pink Diamond' (double bright pink flowers, Zone 5), 'PJM' (single lavender-pink flowers, Zone 4), and 'Olga Mezitt' (single clear pink flowers, Zone 4). These three bloom in sequence from April into May and are open, upright shrubs 4 to 6 feet tall with small, leathery, semi-evergreen leaves that turn

The fuzzy catkins of pussy willow (Salix caprea) are an early sign of spring outdoors and are very easy to force for even earlier bloom indoors.

maroon or bronzy in cold weather. 'Pioneer' (pink-purple flowers, Zone 4) and 'Pioneer Silvery Pink' (clear pink flowers, Zone 5) are compact shrubs 3 to 5 feet tall, blooming in April or May, with small leathery leaves that turn bright red, orange, and pink before dropping in late fall. *Rhododendron mucronulatum* 'Cornell Pink', a deciduous shrub 3 to 5 feet tall, has clear pink flowers at forsythia time. Zone 4.

CULTURE: These rhododendrons tolerate part shade but need plenty of sun for best bloom and foliage color. They require acid, well-drained soil amended with plenty of organic matter and a mulch of pine needles, bark chips, or composted leaves. On a suitable site, they are care-free and long-lived. Shear or prune, if desired, immediately after the flowers drop.

■ *Salix caprea* / **French pussy willow**

DESCRIPTION: Soft, silky, pinkish gray pussy willow catkins are one of the first signs of spring in northern climates. Male and female flowers are borne on separate plants; the males have larger, showier catkins frosted with glowing yellow stamens. Nurseries usually sell the male plants. French pussy willow grows quickly and can develop into a multistemmed tree 15 to 25 feet tall. Regular pruning keeps it shrub-sized. There are other kinds of pussy willows, including a weeping form. Zone 4.

CULTURE: Full sun. Average garden soil and watering. Adapts well to wet sites, but doesn't require constant moisture. If you buy pussy willows from a florist, you can root them in a jar of water or stick them directly into the ground. Pussy willows grow fast and look best if you prune them hard every year or two right after they bloom but before the leaves expand, cutting some or all of the stems down to the ground.

FRAGRANT EARLY-FLOWERING SHRUBS

The following shrubs include some of the most fragrant of all garden plants, with clear sweet perfumes that signal the coming of spring. You may not find them at local garden centers, but they are readily available from mail-order nurseries. It's definitely worth seeking them out if you love fragrant flowers.

- *Abeliophyllum distichum* / White forsythia

An uncommon but desirable deciduous shrub that resembles forsythia but has lightly scented clear white flowers. Grows 3 to 5 feet tall. Sun or part shade, average soil. Zone 4.

- *Corylopsis* spp. / Winter hazels

These deciduous shrubs have dangling clusters of yellow flowers in early spring and attractive foliage later. *Corylopsis glabrescens,* the most hardy species, grows 12 feet tall or taller. *C. pauciflora,* the most commonly available species, grows 4 to 6 feet tall. *C. spicata,* the most beautiful species, grows 6 to 8 feet tall. Full or part sun. Good garden soil. Zone 5.

- *Daphne* spp. / Daphnes

All daphnes have clusters of small but deliciously fragrant flowers. *Daphne caucasica* is deciduous, 4 to 6 feet tall, with white flowers. Zone 5. *D. cneorum* is evergreen, under 1 foot tall but 3 to 4 feet wide, with pink flowers. Zone 4. *D. mezereum* is deciduous, 2 to 3 feet tall, with magenta or sometimes white flowers and bright red berries in summer. Zone 4. All need part sun and well-drained soil.

- *Lindera benzoin* / Spicebush

An adaptable native shrub with clusters of small golden flowers. The flowers, leaves, twigs, and berries are all spicy-scented. Deciduous. Grows 6 to 10 feet tall. Sun or shade. Average or damp soil. Zone 5.

- *Lonicera fragrantissima* / Winter honeysuckle

A vigorous shrub with creamy white lemon-scented flowers, red berries in summer, and foliage that lasts partway into the winter. Prune every year right after it blooms to keep it compact. Otherwise it may grow to 10 feet tall and wide. Full or part sun. Average soil. Zone 5.

- *Ribes* spp. / Currants

Ribes odoratum, buffalo or clove currant, and *R. aureum,* golden currant, have gold flowers with a spicy, clovelike aroma. Both grow 3 to 6 feet tall and adapt

Forcing Shoots for Indoor Bloom

Boughs from the following trees and shrubs make lovely late winter arrangements. Cut them three to five weeks before they would bloom outdoors and put them in a pail of water in a cool, sunny room. Wait a week or so for the buds to swell and show color before making the final arrangement and bringing it into the warmer part of the house.

Abeliophyllum distichum,
   white forsythia

Chaenomeles spp., flowering quinces

Cornus mas, Cornelian cherry
   dogwood

Daphne mezereum, daphne

Forsythia cvs., forsythias

Hamamelis cvs., witch hazels

Magnolia spp., magnolias

Prunus cvs., flowering cherries

Salix spp., pussy willows

Viburnum carlesii, V. × juddii,
   Korean spice viburnums

A bouquet of forced forsythias reassures that spring is near.

Korean spice viburnum (Viburnum carlesii) *blooms about the same time as forsythias. It has pink buds that open into white flowers with a wonderful spicy aroma.*

well to dry soil. Zone 4. *R. sanguineum,* flowering currant, blooms earlier and has more showy pink or red flowers but is scentless and only hardy to Zone 6. It grows up to 12 feet tall and prefers moist soil.

- *Sarcococca hookerana* **var. *humilis* / Sweet box**

Although slow-spreading, this makes an excellent evergreen groundcover, under 18 inches tall, with tiny white flowers that smell like honey. Needs part or full shade and rich, well-drained soil. Hardy on protected sites in Zone 5.

- *Viburnum carlesii* **and related hybrids / Korean spice viburnums**

Viburnum carlesii itself is a popular and adaptable shrub with large hemispherical clusters of very sweet-scented white flowers. The hybrids 'Cayuga' and 'Mohawk' are even better plants, with rosy pink buds that catch your eye weeks

Early Spring Bulbs

Plant dozens of the following inexpensive, early-blooming bulbs under and around deciduous shrubs, in perennial flowerbeds, or even in the lawn. They bloom year after year and multiply quickly to form colorful patches.

Chionodoxa gigantea, **Glory of the snow**.
Clusters of star-shaped flowers in shades of blue, white, or pink. 4 inches tall.

Crocus chrysanthus, **Snow crocus or bunch-flowering crocus**.
These are the earliest crocuses, with white, gold, blue, or violet flowers. Large-flowering crocus bloom a few weeks later but still precede daffodils and tulips. 4 inches tall.

Eranthus hyemalis, **Winter aconite**.
Bright yellow, buttercup-like flowers with a ruff of dark green leaves. 4 inches tall.

Galanthus nivalis, **Snowdrop**.
Bright white flowers that dangle like earrings. 4 inches tall.

Narcissus, **Daffodils**.
'February Gold', 'Little Gem', 'Peeping Tom', and 'Tete-a-tete' are among the earliest daffodils. All have bright yellow flowers and are under 6 inches tall.

Scilla sibirica, **Siberian squill**.
Short spikes of starry blue or white flowers. 5 inches tall.

Snowdrops (Galanthus nivalis) *are white as snow and tough as nails; undaunted by cold, they bloom for weeks in late winter.*

before the flowers open and healthy foliage that resists mildew and looks good all summer. All grow to about 5 feet tall, with a rounded habit. Needs full sun, good garden soil. Zone 5.

PRECOCIOUS PERENNIALS

These low-growing perennials start blooming as soon as the snow melts — sometimes even earlier! Put some of them near the house, where you'll pass them every day on the way to the car or the mailbox, or outside a window so you can see them from indoors. Plant others at the far corner of your lot as a destination, somewhere to go on sunny days when you want to walk outdoors and explore for signs of spring.

■ *Helleborus* spp. / Hellebores

DESCRIPTION: These slow-growing but very long-lived perennials form clumps of leathery evergreen foliage and bear clusters of papery-textured flowers that last for many weeks. The most popular and widely available species are *Helleborus foetidus,* stinking hellebore (clusters of pale green flowers, 1 inch wide, in winter); *H. niger,* Christmas rose (round white flowers, 2 to 4 inches wide, in winter); and *H. orientalis,* Lenten rose (nodding pink, rose, maroon, white, or greenish flowers, in early spring). All grow 18 to 24 inches tall and spread gradually by offsets and seeds to form a small patch. Zone 4.

CULTURE: Part sun or shade. Well-drained, fertile soil. Trim off damaged leaves in late winter. Once hellebores are established, don't disturb them. If you want more plants, look for volunteer seedlings and transplant them when young.

■ *Primula* spp. / Primroses

DESCRIPTION: Primroses bear showy flowers that last for weeks in cool weather. Some of the earliest are *Primula denticulata,* drumstick primrose (scentless lavender, pink, rose, or white flowers); *P. polyantha,* polyanthus primrose (lightly scented flowers in all colors, solid or two-tone); *P. veris,* cowslip (fragrant golden yellow flowers); and *P. vulgaris,* common primrose (fragrant pale yellow flowers). All are small plants, with flower stalks 8 to 12 inches tall and leafy rosettes 8 to 12 inches wide. Zone 5.

Lenten rose (Helleborus orientalis) *is a long-lived, trouble-free perennial with clusters of cup-shaped white, pink, or rose flowers in early spring.*

Pasque flower (Pulsatilla vulgaris) *has anemone-like flowers, fluffy seed heads, and lacy foliage covered with fine silky hairs.*

CULTURE: Primroses grow well under deciduous trees, where they get part sun in spring, shade in summer. They need moist, well-drained, fertile soil amended with plenty of organic matter. Water regularly during summer dry spells. Divide every year or two right after they bloom.

■ *Pulmonaria* spp. / Lungworts

DESCRIPTION: Lungworts start blooming as soon as the snow melts, with masses of small blue, pink, or white flowers that last for several weeks. Rosettes of plain green or silver-spotted leaves expand as the flowers fade. The leaves look good all summer if soil is moist but may die down in hot weather; either way, new leaves develop in fall and last into the winter. There are many fine cultivars. All have flower stalks under 1 foot tall and form rosettes about 1 foot wide. Zone 3.

CULTURE: Part shade or shade. Moist, well-drained soil. Cut off flower stalks when the petals drop. Divide every few years in late summer or early fall.

■ *Pulsatilla* **spp. / Pasque flower**

DESCRIPTION: Pushing up through the snow at Eastertime or earlier, pasque flowers have big fuzzy buds, bell-shaped flowers, finely cut foliage, and fluffy seed heads. *Pulsatilla patens,* native to the western United States, has violet flowers. Common pasque flower, *P. vulgaris,* is more commonly available and has blue-purple, reddish, or white flowers. Under 1 foot tall. Zone 4.

CULTURE: Full sun. Well-drained soil. Care-free.

■ *Sanguinaria canadensis* **/ Bloodroot**

DESCRIPTION: This woodland wildflower is easy to grow and readily available at nurseries. Once established, it spreads and self-sows to form a lovely patch with bright white flowers in early spring and unusual lobed leaves later. Only 8 inches tall, it can spread 18 inches or wider. Zone 4.

CULTURE: Part sun in spring, shade in summer. Well-drained garden soil with plenty of organic matter. Divide every few years in spring if you want to make more plants.

■ *Viola odorata* **/ Sweet violet**

DESCRIPTION: A care-free groundcover for moist, partly shady sites. Sweet violet blooms for several weeks in early spring and again in late fall. There are cultivars with purple, blue, violet, or pink flowers. The vigorous plants have almost-evergreen foliage, stay under 8 inches tall, and spread quickly by runners and seeds to form a patch. Zone 4.

CULTURE: Part sun or shade. Moist, well-drained soil. Divide every year or two in spring or late summer if you want to make more plants.

HARDINESS ZONE MAP

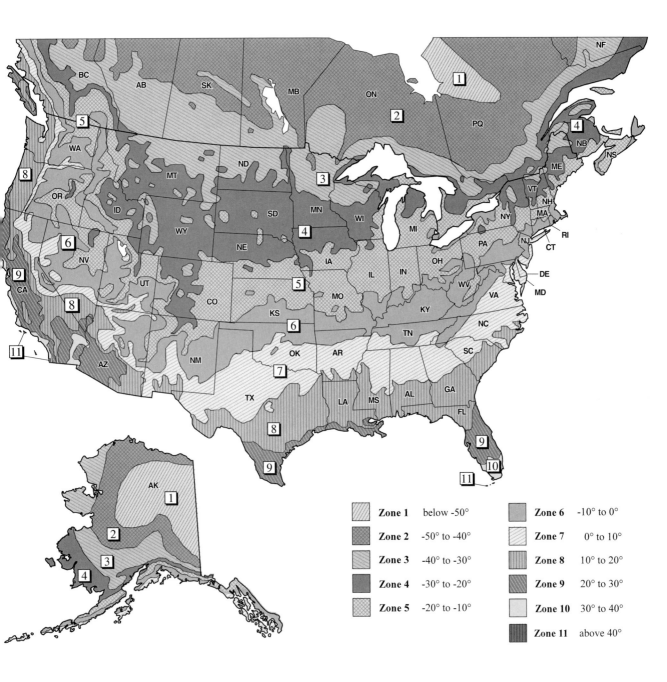

	Zone 1	below -50°		Zone 6	-10° to 0°
	Zone 2	-50° to -40°		Zone 7	0° to 10°
	Zone 3	-40° to -30°		Zone 8	10° to 20°
	Zone 4	-30° to -20°		Zone 9	20° to 30°
	Zone 5	-20° to -10°		Zone 10	30° to 40°
				Zone 11	above 40°

Photo Credits

Cathy Wilkinson Barash: 51, 58, 101

Gay Baumgarner/Photo/Nats: 90

Rita Buchanan: 15 top, 19, 20, 21, 25, 30, 32, 37, 38, 41, 43, 44, 47, 56, 61, 64, 68, 88

David Cavagnaro: iii, 16, 66, 102, 107

R. Todd Davis: 69, 74, 99

Derek Fell: vi–1, 5, 8, 13, 27, 29, 35, 36, 48, 59, 76, 85, 92, 109, 110

Charles Marden Fitch: 17, 26, 53, 63, 80, 96, 98

Rick Mastelli: 6, 23, 86, 89, 105, 112

John Neubauer: 73, 79, back cover

Jerry Pavia: 15 bottom, 71, 83, 95, 106

Patricia Taylor: 11

RECOMMENDED READING

Color for Your Winter Yard and Garden with Flowers, Berries, Birds and Trees. Helen Van Pelt Wilson. New York: Scribner's, 1978.

Colour in the Winter Garden, rev. ed. Graham Stuart Thomas. Portland, Oregon: Timber Press, 1994.

The Garden in Winter. Rosemary Verey. Boston: Little, Brown, 1988.

Taylor's Master Guide to Gardening. Rita Buchanan and Roger Holmes, eds. Boston: Houghton Mifflin, 1994.

The Undaunted Garden. Lauren Springer. Golden, Colorado: Fulcrum Press, 1994.

The Unsung Season. Sydney Eddison. Boston: Houghton Mifflin, 1995.

The Winter Garden. Erica Glasener, guest ed. New York: Brooklyn Botanic Garden, 1991.

A Year at North Hill. Joe Eck and Wayne Winterrowd. New York: Henry Holt, 1995.

INDEX

Titles available in the Taylor's Weekend Gardening Guides series:

Organic Pest and Disease Control	$12.95
Safe and Easy Lawn Care	12.95
Window Boxes	12.95
Attracting Birds and Butterflies	12.95
Water Gardens	12.95
Easy, Practical Pruning	12.95
The Winter Garden	12.95
Backyard Building Projects	12.95
Indoor Gardens	12.95
Plants for Problem Places	12.95

At your bookstore or by calling 1-800-225-3362

Prices subject to change without notice